CAMPAIGNING AGAINST CRUELTY

The hundred year history of the British Union for the Abolition of Vivisection

Emma Hopley

BUAV
*campaigning to end
animal experiments*

British Union for the Abolition of Vivisection
16a Crane Grove, London, N7 8LB

First published 1998 by The British Union of Abolition, 16a Crane Grove,
London, N7 8LB. Tel: 0171-700 4888. Fax: 0171-700 0252.

A catalogue record for this book is available from the British Library.

ISBN 1 870356 16 0

Packaged for the BUAV by Gary Andersen-Jones @ EAJ Licensing Ltd.
Design by Joel Chernin.

Origination - Graphic Ideas, London, N1.
Printed in China by Regent Publishing Services.

The Sending of the Animals

The Animals, you say, were "sent"
For man's free use and nutriment.
Pray, then, inform me, and be candid,
Why came they aeons before man did,
To spend long centuries on earth,
Awaiting their devourer's birth?
Those ill-timed chattels, sent from Heaven,
Were, sure, the maddest gift e'er given -
"Sent" for Man's usage (can Man believe it?)
When there was no man to receive it!

Henry Salt (1851 to 1939)

Reproduced from *The Savour of Salt: A Henry Salt Anthology* with the kind permission of Centaur Press Ltd

Preface

This book has been written to commemorate the centenary year of the British Union for the Abolition of Vivisection (BUAV) and its 100 years of continuous campaigning to bring about an end to animal experimentation. BUAV was not the first anti-vivisection society to be established, yet it has become the largest and best recognised society of its kind in the world. Its founder and President, Frances Power Cobbe, is recognised as the pioneer of the anti-vivisection movement.

The original and only objective of the society is the 'abolition of vivisection without compromise of any kind'; these words were written into the Constitution of the society with the instruction that they were not to be altered. While BUAV cannot declare itself to have achieved its ultimate objective of ending animal experiments, it certainly lays claim to having elevated the issue onto the public, political, philosophical, scientific and theological agendas of the day. It will continue to do this work as long as the need remains.

Throughout its history BUAV has collected and stored documentation and data in relation to the organisation and now boasts an archive collection which is one of the finest of its kind in the world. In 1993, in recognition of the value of the collection, BUAV found a home for its records at the Brynmor Jones Library at the University of Hull where specialist facilities will help to preserve the documents for generations to come. The collection contains a wide range of documents, from annual reports and minute books to photographs and old film footage and is now available to bona fide researchers.

About the author

Emma Hopley was born in Stockport in 1969. She was brought up in the small village of High Lane on the edge of the Greater Manchester/Cheshire border. She was educated at Marple Ridge High School and graduated from Sheffield University with a BA Hons Degree (History) in 1988. Trained as a librarian, she has been employed in this capacity at BUAV since July 1995. She is both a member of BUAV and a supporter of animal rights. She currently lives in Walthamstow, London, with her husband Paul Murphy.

Acknowledgements

I would like to thank the following people for their input into the production of this book, however large or small: all my friends and colleagues at BUAV, especially Kathy Roddy and Matthew Davis; Brian Dyson and Hilary Marsh from the Brynmor Jones Library at the University of Hull for their work with the BUAV archive collection; Dr Lori Williamson of Oxford Brookes University for biographical details of Frances Power Cobbe; Twiggy Lawson for contributing the foreword; and my husband, Paul Murphy, for moral support and encouragement.

Every effort has been made to trace the copyright of all photographs and illustrations used. The publishers apologise for any errors, and would welcome these being brought to their attention. We are most grateful to the following for waiving their copyright fees to reproduce pictures: Mary Evans Picture Library and the Royal Commission on the Historical Monuments of England.

Abbreviations used

1876 Act	Cruelty to Animals Act 1876
1986 Act	Animals (Scientific Procedures) Act 1986
AAMR	Association for the Advancement of Medicine by Research
AGM	annual general meeting
ALF	Animal Liberation Front
BBC	British Broadcasting Corporation
BIBRA	British Industrial Biological Research Association
BMA	British Medical Association
BUAV	British Union for the Abolition of Vivisection
CIWF	Compassion in World Farming
EGM	emergency general meeting
FRAME	Fund for the Replacement of Animals in Medical Experiments
HLS	Huntingdon Life Sciences
HRC	Huntingdon Research Centre
ICI	Imperial Chemical Industries
MRC	Medical Research Council
NAVS	National Anti-Vivisection Society
NCDL	National Canine Defence League
NGRC	National Greyhound Racing Club
RCS	Royal College of Surgeons of England
RDS	Research Defence Society
RSPCA	Royal Society for the Prevention of Cruelty to Animals

Contents list

Foreword

As a friend of the British Union for the Abolition of Vivisection, which I have supported for many years, I am delighted to write the foreword to this book. *Campaigning Against Cruelty* is an enthralling account of the fight against the suffering caused to laboratory animals.

Written to mark the centenary of BUAV, the inspiration for so many initiatives in response to the abuse of animals around the world, the book provides an historical account of the organisation from its foundation in 1898, to the present day with its sophisticated campaigning and lobbying work.

Emma Hopley begins the story of BUAV with an account of the founder Frances Power Cobbe, an extraordinary and inspiring woman who not only founded BUAV but was also a prominent supporter of women's rights. Emma then describes in fascinating detail the successes and the setbacks as, over the years, the organisation attracts both mass support and fierce opposition. Fascinating stories are revealed such as the 'Brown Dog Affair', the trial of Dr Hadwen, the fight against compulsory vaccination, the supply of pet animals to laboratories and hazardous undercover investigations.

My great hope is that there will be no need to commemorate BUAV's second centenary; by then, hopefully, this cruel and scientifically flawed practice will be outlawed thanks to the campaigning work of organisations like BUAV.

Until then, this book serves as a timely reminder of what goes on behind closed doors and I wholeheartedly recommend it to the countless thousands of people across the world committed to the protection of animals.

Twiggy Lawson
February 1998

CHAPTER 1

The prelude years 1863 to 1898

The emergence of an anti-vivisection movement

Reports of horses being used in French veterinary schools for the practice of surgical techniques moved Frances Power Cobbe to write one of her first anti-vivisection tracts. This picture shows the Royal Veterinary College in 1891

Early opposition to laboratory medicine

Vivisection was not entirely new in the 1870s but up until that time it had always been regarded as a continental practice. Laboratories in France and Germany were developing laboratory medicine at a much greater rate than in Britain as medical research at home attracted hardly any state funding and did not lead to academic status in universities. The early practitioners were not without their critics. In 1758 Samuel Johnson deplored the fact that animal experiments were 'being published every day with ostentation' by doctors who 'extend the arts of torture', but it cannot be said that there was any form of organised opposition.

But by the 1870s a small number of British physiologists were actively promoting continental experimen-tal methods at home and the *Handbook for the Physiological Laboratory* (edited by Burdon-Sanderson), first published in English in 1873, revealed the similarities between practices in Britain and abroad. Agitation from the anti-vivisectionists developed and between 1875 and 1900 vivisection was to become

the touchstone to test the attitude as to our duty towards the animal creation.[1]

Vivisection became a major public issue and an organised opposition movement emerged in the last quarter of the 19th century. Legislation was eventually passed in Britain regulating the practice, the only country to do so before the 20th century.

Frances Power Cobbe (1822 to 1904): 'the head of the battle against vivisection'

One woman who was to play a major role in the anti-vivisection movement was Frances Power Cobbe. Cobbe first became aware of the practice of vivisection in 1863 when her travels across Europe brought her into contact with it. Two events occurred during this year which were to set her on a career as an anti-vivisectionist, a passion that was to occupy her for the rest of her life and earn her the title

the head of the battle against vivisection in England.[2]

Frances Power Cobbe, founder of BUAV and pioneer of the anti-vivisection movement, 1894

The first of these events was the discovery of a newspaper article about the teaching practices at a veterinary school in Alfort, France, where unanaesthetised horses were used to practise surgical techniques. In response she wrote 'The Rights of Man and the Claims of Brutes' which was published in *Fraser's Magazine*, and later reprinted as an anti-vivisection pamphlet. This was to be her first opposition to the practice of vivisection, and Cobbe believed it to be the first attempt to deal with the moral aspect of vivisection. Her opposition would eventually lead to the foundation of an anti-vivisectionist organisation, based on the principle of abolition - the British Union for the Abolition of Vivisection. In the 40 years in which Cobbe campaigned tirelessly against vivisection, she did 'raise considerably' the 'claims' of animals as set out in her original tract and accorded them 'rights'.

While Cobbe was visiting Florence in Italy later that year, an acquaintance, Dr Appleton of Harvard University, drew her attention to the experiments of a Professor Schiff. Appleton told Cobbe how he had seen dogs, pigeons, and other creatures in a 'mangled and suffering' condition in Schiff's laboratory. Cobbe drafted a petition that was sent round Florence and was eventually presented to Schiff with 783 signatures, although he seems to have paid little or no heed to it. It did however cause the subject to be much discussed and

paved the way for the complaints and lawsuits concerning the 'nuisances' of the moaning dogs which followed. These eventually made Florence an unpleasant place for Schiff and he retreated to Geneva in 1877.

Frances Power Cobbe was born in Dublin in December 1822 into a typical upper class family. Following the death of her mother in 1847 she took over the domestic duties at the family home in Newbridge and 10 years later, after her father died, she set off on an 11-month tour of Europe and the Middle East. On her return she found herself without any real purpose in life; an increasing number of upper class women in similar circumstances became known as 'redundant women'.

Cobbe set about establishing herself a career as a philanthropist. Beginning with the problem of Bristol's waifs and strays she also concerned herself with reform of the workhouses, the rights of women and eventually those of animals. She combined her philanthropic activities with a journalistic and literary career, including articles for the *Daily News* and *Echo* newspapers and popular magazines of the day, and wrote several books, including her autobiography.

Ethical arguments ... moral and sentient interests

Cobbe was not an advocate of what we know today as 'animal rights' (she was not a vegetarian) but she did believe that man's relationship with animals was based on moral grounds. She argued that whereas animals only had sentient interests, man had both moral and sentient interests, and that moral interests should take precedence over sentient ones. She believed that it was acceptable for man to use animals to satisfy his needs, for food for example, but not to inflict unnecessary suffering on them.

These moral arguments were in accordance with Cobbe's religious beliefs which essentially were that it was man's duty to God to treat his creatures mercifully. She likened God to an umpire who might accept the

Frances Power Cobbe, 1879

need to kill animals for food, and to prevent their threat to humans, but such an umpire would never sanction killing for sport or vivisection.

Frances Power Cobbe did not deny that vivisection had provided man with knowledge in the past, or that it was possible it might again in the future. But she did not believe this should be accepted as a basis to allow the practice to continue. She did not believe that the advancement of science could be justified by the means from which it was obtained; she believed, in other words, that the good of mankind did not justify the 'torture of beasts'.

Legislative protection of animals

The only legal protection accorded to animals was the Animal Protection Act of 1822 which became known as Martin's Act after its originator Richard Martin, MP for Galway. This Act, which coincidentally came into force the same year that Cobbe was born, protected horses and cattle against cruelty and improper treatment. Its important feature was that it assumed the principle that cruelty to animals was wrong and of over 40,000 offenders who were prosecuted under its provisions not one attempted to protest over the principle on which it was founded.

Cobbe, however, questioned the effectiveness of Martin's Act as a basis for prosecution in vivisection cases following the unsuccessful attempt by the Royal Society for the Prevention of Cruelty to Animals (RSPCA) in 1874 to prosecute against cruelty to dogs that had been experimented on. The French physiologist Eugène Magnan had induced epileptic fits in two dogs by injecting them with alcohol and absinthe at the annual meeting of the British Medical Association (BMA) in Norwich. John Colam, Secretary of the RSPCA, used Martin's Act in an attempt to prosecute Magnan and the two British doctors who had condoned his actions. It was however unsuccessful and Magnan

Richard Martin MP ('Humanity Dick')

RSPCA

hastily withdrew to his home country.

The fight for legislative regulation

Frances Power Cobbe saw the need for further protection of all 'God's creatures', and not just horses and cattle as defined in the Act. She wrote two pamphlets on this issue - *Need of a Bill* and *Reasons for Interference* - and urged the RSPCA to become more directly involved in opposition to vivisection by using the Act for further test cases and to support the prohibition of painful experiments. She emphasised the alarming rate at which vivisection was increasing in Britain and suggested that the incident in Norwich was merely the tip of the iceberg.

Her expectations from the RSPCA were not met and so a Bill was drawn up to regulate vivisection with the help of her anti-vivisectionist friend Dr George Hoggan and various sympathetic politicians. The Bill was presented to the House of Lords in May 1875 but was quickly countered by one from the medical community. The simultaneous introduction of two Bills on the same issue led to the appointment of a Royal Commission to investigate the matter before proceeding any further with legislative action. The Commission was appointed in July 1875 (at which point both the Bills were withdrawn) and its findings reported in January of the following year.

In the meantime, at the suggestion of Dr Hoggan and with his help, Cobbe founded the Society for the Protection of Animals Liable to Vivisection, later renamed the Victoria Street Society. Lord Shaftesbury, an influential ally of Cobbe's, was President while Cobbe herself was Honorary Secretary. The launch of this anti-vivisection campaign was to become a personal crusade for Cobbe and was to occupy the rest of her life.

In March 1876 Cobbe was installed at the Society's headquarters at 20 Victoria Street. She records that as soon as she was left alone in the office she

resolved never to go to bed at night leaving a stone unturned which might help to stop vivisection[3]

and she later reflected in her autobiography that she believed herself

to have kept that resolution [4]

She decorated the office with pictures and hung curtains in order to make it as cheerful as possible for visitors in order not to distress them over the 'frightful' nature of the work.

Accepting the need for 'legislative interference'

The first Royal Commission, reporting in January 1876, concluded that it was not desirable to prohibit experiments on animals, but did accept the need for 'legislative interference'. It thought that by making the practice illegal it would only be driven underground, or that the medical and physiological students of Britain would move abroad. It saw the compulsory use of anaesthetics as a solution - to prevent pain, or at least greatly reduce it.

The Commission realised the need for reconciliation between the desire for scientific knowledge and the sentiment of humanity, as science alone could not be the judge of this. The most notable evidence of this came from a Dr Klein who, in reply to a question from the Chairman of the Commission, answered that with respect to animal suffering he had 'no regard at all'.[5]

A further restrictionist Bill was introduced into the House of Lords by Lord Carnarvon on 15 May 1876 based on the notion that vivisection could be controlled by proper legislation. The Bill followed most of the recommendations put forward by the Victoria Street Society including making scientists accountable for their actions. However, the medical community saw this as an attack on their integrity and set out to oppose it.

Opposition by the medical profession

The Bill had almost completed its passage through Parliament when, at a critical point, Lord Carnarvon, in whose hands it lay, was called away from London by

Martin's Act was used to bring cases of cruelty to animals to court but Cobbe argued that it did not offer sufficient protection to laboratory animals

the illness and subsequent death of his mother. A deputation of medical professionals seized their opportunity and presented a petition of over 3,000 signatures asking the Home Secretary to make modifications to the Bill. On 15 August 1876 a modified Bill received royal assent, becoming the Cruelty to Animals Act 1876. The last-minute amendments though were substantial enough to alter its fundamental nature as it allowed nearly all of the restrictions imposed to be annulled by means of exemption certificates. Lord Carnarvon's Bill, which had been intended to protect animals, was transformed in his absence and without his knowledge into a law which imposed no real restrictions on vivisection.

Those who had initiated and supported the Bill were deeply disappointed, none more so than Frances Power Cobbe for whom

the world has never seemed to me quite the same since that dreadful time.[6]

The anti-vivisectionists regarded the Act as no more than a charter for vivisectionists but were urged by Lord Shaftesbury to accept it as a framework on which subsequent amendments could be made. However when the Act was eventually superseded 110 years later by the Animals (Scientific Procedures) Act of 1986 it had not been amended once.

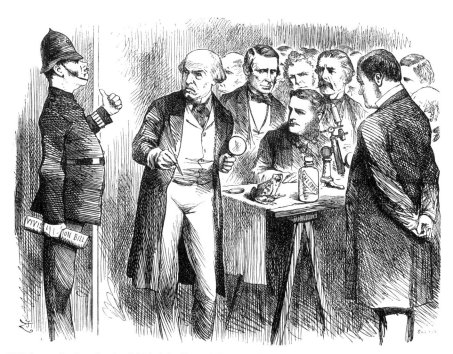

In July 1876 the medical profession lobbied the Home Office to defend its right to vivisect (Reproduced by permission of Punch Ltd)

Moving from a policy of restriction to one of abolition

In response to their disillusionment, members of the Victoria Street Society became convinced that animal experiments could not be regulated by legislation, the medical profession was not to be trusted and politicians too had proved themselves unreliable. The Society therefore voted on 22 November 1876 in favour of moving from a policy of restriction to one of abolition. A Bill was drawn up which was debated in the House of Commons but was voted out by 83 to 222 votes. This did not come as a surprise to the Society and it set about appealing to public opinion to convince them of the immorality of vivisection in the hope that a massive public outcry would result in the practice being prohibited by law.

The Society set up a journal in 1881, *The Zoophilist*, which Cobbe edited for a while. It published a large number of books, pamphlets and leaflets many of which were written by Cobbe. In 1884 she retired to Wales with her close friend Mary Lloyd and although she had resigned her post as Honorary Secretary she retained her membership of the Society and attended meetings when possible.

Cobbe's retirement was to be short lived. At a Council meeting in February 1898 the Society, which was now known as the National Anti-Vivisection Society (NAVS) and under the leadership of Stephen Coleridge, passed a resolution that:

While the demand for the total abolition of vivisection will ever remain the ultimate object of the National Anti-Vivisection Society, the society is not thereby precluded from making efforts in Parliament for lesser measures, having for their object the saving of animals from scientific tortures.[7]

Frances Power Cobbe opposed the resolution; she could not condone Coleridge's policy of 'lesser measures'. In protest, she and some of the older members resigned their membership. Later that year Cobbe founded the British Union for the Abolition of Vivisection, an anti-vivisection society founded on the principle of total abolition.

CHAPTER 2

1898 to 1904

'Ploughing the ground' - raising awareness of vivisection

Development of a union to oppose vivisection

The British Union for the Abolition of Vivisection, originally known as the British Union, or simply the Union, was founded at a public meeting on 14 June 1898 in Bristol. Frances Power Cobbe, the founder, also took the position of President, a post that she was to hold right up to her death. Other key posts were held by Mrs Roscoe (Honorary Secretary), Miss Florence Baker (Secretary) and John Freeman Norris (Treasurer).

The British Union, as its name suggested, was to be a union of anti-vivisection societies. Some existing anti-vivisection societies converted to become branches of the Union, while others remained independent but became part of the federation. New branches were also established. The Central Section of the Union was the Bristol and West of England Anti-Vivisection Society whose offices formed the original headquarters of the Union.

Five anti-vivisection societies were immediately incorporated into the Union; these were the Bristol and West of England Anti-Vivisection Society, the Electoral Anti-Vivisection League, York Anti-Vivisection Society, Macclesfield Anti-Vivisection Society and Liverpool and District Anti-Vivisection Society. The number of branches grew steadily over the years reaching a peak in 1940 when there were no fewer than 154 branches, including six in Australia and one in New Zealand.

A half-year report produced in October 1898 recognised that establishment of a journal of its own must be a priority for the Union. *The Zoophilist*, published by NAVS, refused to publicise the British Union's meetings

Dr Walter Hadwen, BUAV President 1910 to 1932

and announcements as it did for other anti-vivisection societies. The first edition of the Union's journal - *The Abolitionist* - appeared on 15 April 1899 and was edited by John Verschoyle.

Cobbe had heard of the 'firebrand' anti-vaccinationist Dr Walter Hadwen of Gloucester and was tempted to make use of his oratory skill on her own platform. But she hesitated for a long time. The anti-vivisection movement was still in its infancy and she did not want to risk alienating her distinguished supporters by association with the anti-vaccination movement, which was essentially seen as a working class movement.

Cobbe sent a 'spy' to Gloucester from whom she learnt of the high local esteem in which Hadwen was held so she took the plunge and Dr Hadwen was invited. He proved to be a great asset to the society. He spoke at the Union's meetings, contributed articles to *The Abolitionist* and, after Verschoyle's death, he became the anonymous and unpaid editor of the journal for the next 20 years. Eventually he succeeded Cobbe as President of the Union in 1910.

The aim of the Union was originally defined as:

To keep unalterably before its members and the public the fundamental principle of their warfare with scientific cruelty, namely, that it is a great Sin - which can only be opposed effectively when opposed absolutely, and without attempts at delusive compromises of any kind.[8]

The British Union hoped to convince the nation of the

A typical BUAV campaign shop (Bristol 1911) with Nurse Cross, the BUAV organiser in the doorway

cruelty of vivisection and to expose the false statements of its supporters, in particular the notion that vivisection in Britain did not involve cruelty because of the use of anaesthetics. They argued that it was not just the actual cutting involved in an operation that caused cruelty but also the days and weeks afterwards of the recovery period during which the animal would suffer. They suggested that to make the claim that torture did not take place in British laboratories because of the use of anaesthetics was in fact

to play with words and to make a deliberate attempt to deceive the public.[9]

The public had to be convinced of the existence of the cruelty of vivisection as this was the first step to abolishing it.

In addition to the moral arguments there was also the scientific standpoint that vivisection was in fact an unscientific practice. The anatomical and physiological differences between man and other animals meant that any results obtained from experiments on animals were not reliable and could not be extrapolated to humans.

Raising awareness of the cruelty of vivisection: campaigns gather momentum

The British Union embarked on a campaign to educate and inform the public of the reality of experimentation on animals. The branches undertook the campaigning work, which was reported in the monthly pages of *The Abolitionist*.

One particularly successful method of capturing public attention was the renting of vacant shops in town centres for weeks at a time. A short-term lease would be agreed and then the shop would be stocked with leaflets and publications, with posters displayed in the windows to attract passers-by. The shops were staffed by a supporter who was on hand to answer questions.

Mrs Mabel Cook, Honorary Secretary of the North of England branch, had been the 'ingenious devisor of this plan' and ran the first of these shops in Wrexham, Bangor and Barmouth. Reports of one of the earliest shops in Wrexham described how anti-vivisection literature was handed out and how, day after day, a constant stream of visitors, both friends and foes, passed in and out of the shop asking questions, offering suggestions, raising objections or entering into debate. Tickets were handed out for a public meeting to be held the following month by which time the whole town had been 'thoroughly canvassed and awakened'. Over 1,000 people attended the packed meeting to listen to Dr Hadwen and the local MP speak.

The technique quickly became such a success as a way of arousing public interest that the Union noted that it would be desirable for all its offices to be located in prime spots in the town, on a ground floor and with windows opening onto 'well-frequented streets'. It was agreed that the central office, currently located on the first floor of 20 The Triangle, Bristol, should be moved to a more appropriate site to conform with these guidelines.

Shops opened in towns throughout England and Wales, and later in Scotland too. By the end of 1914 there had already been over 80 shop campaigns.

Other campaigning methods included public meetings in towns throughout England and Wales for which lecturers were employed; letter-writing to the press in order to raise the level of debate; distribution of *The Abolitionist* and other publications; and meetings at the headquarters in Bristol during lunchtimes. This work was what Frances Power Cobbe referred to as 'ploughing the ground' - an essential preparatory step on the road to legislative moral reform.

The anti-vivisection movement: a leadership role for women

Women played a very significant role in the British Union as they did in the anti-vivisection movement in general. Philanthropic and reform movements had provided women with an entry into public life, from which they were generally excluded. But the anti-vivisection movement was unique in that it gave women the opportunity to become involved in the leadership of the organisations to which they belonged.

The first Executive Committee of the Victoria Street Society had five women, eight men and a male President, but the first annual report of the British Union in 1899 shows a female majority on the Executive Committee with Frances Power Cobbe as President. Women also outnumbered men on the list of vice presidents of the Society, although these had much more of a symbolic role.

There were links between the women's movement and the anti-vivisection movement. Cobbe herself had been a supporter of women's access to higher education and the protection of women against violent husbands, and the Married Women's Property Act of 1870 had largely been her work. However, there were some women who supported women's rights but not those of animals, and vice versa. It was the same for male supporters of these two movements. Sir Victor Horsley for example was one of the most despised of all vivisectors yet was known to be a strong advocate of women's suffrage. Conversely Stephen Coleridge, Honorary Secretary of NAVS, did not support women's suffrage.

Some thought the movements to be inextricably linked and warned that, if women got the vote, legal restraint of vivisection would inevitably follow. Hindsight shows that this was not to be the case.

The importance of the work of women in furthering the cause was recognised by the Union as seen in the following passage taken from *The Abolitionist:*

as for all movements of moral reform in our time, women have proved, and are proving, that their help cannot be dispensed with. Where, indeed, should we be in our own special movement - the crusade against vivisection - if we had to work without the aid of women? We should be like a labourer who, in order to help himself digging a plot, tied one hand behind his back.[10]

Women who volunteered for the Union were known as the Band of Service. They distributed literature in the street, helped to run the campaign shops, acted as sandwich board advertisers, helped run fundraising stalls at bazaars and worked in the branch offices. All of this work was undertaken with a 'devotion little short of heroism'.

Campaign against the Brown Institution: the 'headquarters of vivisection in England'

One of the earliest specific campaigns conducted by the Union was that against the Brown Institution which once stood at 149 Wandsworth Road, Vauxhall, in south London. The Union formed its Surrey branch for the sole purpose of conducting this campaign and it pledged to continue its work until vivisection had been abolished from the Institution.

In 1852 Thomas Brown had left a bequest of over £20,000 to the University of London on condition that the Senate should provide an infirmary for sick and suffering animals. The Institution, founded in 1871, had both a hospital and a research laboratory. Immediately following the passing of the Cruelty to Animals Act 1876 the Institution registered with the Home Office enabling it to carry out experiments on living animals.

Thomas Brown had left an extremely detailed will explaining

The Abolitionist **could be bought from members of the Band of Service**

how he wished his money to be spent. The primary purpose was the establishment of a hospital designed partly to treat sick and injured animals but also to carry out research into the nature and cause of animal diseases. It would appear that what he had in mind was research on animals which were already sick, and not the deliberate infliction of disease by scientists.

But a scientific paper published in the *Journal of Pathology and Bacteriology* in February 1900 by Dr Rose-Bradford provided evidence that animals were being used for experimental purposes at the Institution for research into human disease. Furthermore, Thomas Brown had said of the appointed Professor-Superintendent that 'kindness to the animals committed to his charge shall be a general principle of the Institution'. Yet the appointed professor-superintendents included some of the most notorious Victorian vivisectors such

as Victor Horsley, John Rose-Bradford and John Burdon-Sanderson, who wrote his notorious handbook while at the Institution.

Cobbe described the Institution as the 'headquarters of vivisection in England', and it was regarded by the Union as the least defensible point of vivisection as research conducted there was in direct conflict with the original intention of the infirmary, and therefore represented a misappropriation of funds. The Union decided to use an appeal to people's sense of justice. The intention behind the campaign was to expel the vivisectors from the Brown Institution and restore it to its proper use to alleviate animal suffering.

At Cobbe's request an article was written for *The Abolitionist*, which was subsequently reprinted and distributed from door to door in the area around the Institution. A book of signatures was collected from neighbours who could hear the cries of the animals from their homes and wished to protest.

Fifty-three thousand signatures of protest were collected in four months which were presented to the Home Secretary, asking him to withdraw the licences for vivisection from the Institution. The response was disappointing. He claimed that successive home secretaries had granted the licences over many years and that a licence could only be refused on the grounds that the building was not structurally sound or properly equipped. He claimed that any contention over the will was a matter for the law courts, and that if the Institution was a nuisance to neighbours then they should take the necessary formal legal proceedings.

As it was obvious they were not going to get any success from the Home Secretary, Cobbe suggested that they should address a respectful petition to the Senate of the University of London, the trustees of the

Brown Institution. A petition was drafted and included over 200 signatures of influential individuals such as MPs and titled people. The Senate however refused to accept a deputation to present the petition saying that it had to be referred to a committee.

On receiving the report of this committee, the Secretary of the Senate wrote to the Union informing it that the petition had been a 'misapprehension of the facts' and that terms such as 'terrible, painful and revolting', as used in the petition, could not be applied to any experiment carried out at the Institution. Furthermore, all experiments were conducted in accordance with the Cruelty to Animals Act 1876. The Senate concluded that it could see no reason why the administration of the Institution needed regulating and refused to enter into any further debate on the matter.

Unfortunately the campaign against the Brown Institution did not succeed in its aims. In fact the Institution continued with its work and was only closed down when it sustained bomb damage on five separate occasions during the Second World War and was finally destroyed in July 1944 by enemy fire.

The death of Frances Power Cobbe ... a lifetime of campaigning

Frances Power Cobbe died of heart failure on 5 April 1904, aged 81. She was buried three days later in the churchyard at Llanelltyd, Wales, alongside her friend Mary Lloyd who had died several years earlier.

Her funeral was carried out in strict accordance with instructions left in her will. These included that her coffin was not to be made of oak or any durable wood, but of the lightest, most perishable material

merely sufficient to carry my body decently to the grave, and without any ornament or inscription whatever.[11]

She requested that she should be carried to the cemetery in one of her own carriages driven by her own coachman at his usual pace, and that her friends and servants were not to wear mourning dress. These instructions were carried out by Dr Hadwen who had been summoned immediately to Wales at the news of her death.

Her death was reported in all the major newspapers and even the *British Medical Journal* paid tribute to her. *The Daily Star* suggested that she

ought to have a statue in Trafalgar Square, or in St Paul's, or in Westminster Abbey [and] called upon the women of England to enshrine her in the noble company of saints, beside Elizabeth Fry and Florence Nightingale.[12]

Frances Power Cobbe's death had not been unexpected; she was after all 81 years old. But her wish was that her recently formed society, the British Union for the Abolition of Vivisection, would continue her work. This she entrusted to the capable hands of Dr Hadwen with whom she had shared many common sympathies and interests, and who had become a close personal friend. The work of the Union continued almost without abatement as Cobbe would have wished. The only notable delay was that the April edition of *The Abolitionist* appeared five days late as its pages were largely rewritten to pay tribute to the life and work of the Union's founder.

Just a matter of weeks later the Union was to suffer a second loss with the death of its Honorary Treasurer, John Freeman Norris. Norris had been with Frances Power Cobbe in the Union since its beginning and had served as its regular legal adviser as well as lecturing at public meetings and occasionally contributing articles to *The Abolitionist*.

This double loss marked the end of an era which had seen the vigour and courage of one woman's personal crusade, the gradual emergence of public awareness about the horrors of vivisection, intensive campaigning for legislative change, and the establishment of the British Union for the Abolition of Vivisection.

CHAPTER 3

1904 to 1914

Policies and politics: the search for common ground

Increasing parliamentary and propaganda role

One of Cobbe's wishes had been for the Central Section of the Union to be moved from Bristol to London in order to cope with the increasing parliamentary and propaganda work. This was one of the first actions taken, in 1905, a year after her death. The new office was located on the third floor of 32 Charing Cross, opposite the Admiralty. The office was open to the public and Miss Beatrice Kidd, the Secretary, 'welcomed callers' on weekdays from 10am to 5pm and on Saturday mornings. In 1913 the office moved from the third to the first floor of the building which was more convenient for campaigning.

A summary of branch activities was recorded each month in *The Abolitionist*

Vigorous growth of the Union

In the period after Cobbe's death the British Union continued to grow rapidly with new branches becoming incorporated all the time. The Union felt that a marked progress was taking place in the gradual but steady conversion of the public to the principles underlying the anti-vivisection movement, and accredited this to its continual campaigning and educational work. The Union pledged to take advantage of this awakening interest to pursue its mission with increasing vigour.

Membership of the Union had increased to 49 branches by 1912. It believed itself to be the biggest anti-vivisection society in the world, holding in its ranks 'practically all of the oldest pioneers of the movement'. From 1913 the Union also took an office in Manchester (at 39 Victoria Buildings) to facilitate campaigning work in the north.

The growth of the Union and its activities were reflected in the increase in *The Abolitionist* from eight to 20 pages in 1911 and it was given a new and more striking cover. Attempts to keep it to 20 pages were abandoned as impracticable: the magazine often ran to 24 pages because there was always so much information to be included. It could not however exceed 24 pages because of the weight limit of the penny postage. *The Abolitionist* was distributed to libraries

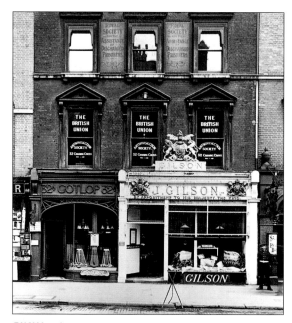

BUAV headquaters moved to London in 1905 and in 1913 occupied the first floor at 32 Charing Cross

Facing page: the front cover of *The Abolitionist,* 1917

THE ABOLITIONIST

THE BRITISH ANTI-VIVISECTION MAGAZINE

ANTI-VIVISECTION

Contents.

Never waste a copy of the Abolitionist, which is a storehouse of information. PUBLICITY WILL END VIVISECTION.

Published by the British Union for the Abolition of Vivisection
(The British Anti-Vivisection Society),
32, CHARING CROSS. S.W

Telegrams:
ABOLITION, LONDON.
Telephone: 8251 CITY

2D.

"No Cruelty is Useful" Cicero.

No. 5.—Vol. XVIII.

May 1, 1917.

and reading rooms where it was on public display. It was also available in WH Smith and members of the Band of Service could be seen selling it on the street.

The number of public meetings held also reflected the increase in public interest in the issue. The annual reports between 1909 and 1914 record an increase in the number of public meetings held from 100 to 260. Locations included open air meetings in parks, public halls, churches, working men's halls and private residences. The Union also organised an annual public meeting which was well attended. At the annual public meeting on 14 May 1909 at Caxton Hall, Westminster, people had to be turned away and many had to stand throughout the proceedings because of lack of space. The meetings were eventually moved to the larger Grand Hall at Kensington Town Hall but the room would often still be packed to overflowing.

Playwright George Bernard Shaw was an anti-vivisectionist

Sketch of George Bernard Shaw speaking at a BUAV public meeting, 1909

and a popular speaker of his time. He addressed several of the Union's annual public meetings and he held his audiences captivated with his wit and eloquence. He ridiculed vivisection with scathing satire. Shaw had leapt to the defence of Cobbe in 1892 following the publication of her book *The Nine Circles of the Hell of the Innocent* when Sir Victor Horsley accused her of omitting information and falsifying facts, and publicly accused her of being a liar. Shaw rendered Horsley speechless when he declared that the question

is not whether Miss Cobbe is a liar but whether you as a vivisector are a scoundrel.[13]

The shop campaigns continued to be an important campaigning technique for spreading the word. Stalls were held at exhibitions and bazaars and events such as

Crufts and the Crystal Palace Dog Show.

Debating classes were held by Miss Kidd on the last Friday of each month at the London office. Their object was to encourage the study of anti-vivisection literature and to educate anti-vivisectionists in the sorts of questions generally raised by opponents. Instruction was given on the legal, historical and medical aspects of vivisection. This method was adopted by several of the branches and some also held evening classes for those 'engaged in business' during the day.

Anti-vivisection contributions were generally well received by newspaper editors who started to open their columns more freely for discussion of the subject. The editor of *The Standard* approached Dr Hadwen to write a series of three articles stating the case against vivisection. The opposing view was to be presented by Stephen Paget. These two men were 'the recognised leading authorities on both sides'.[14] The writings were later published as a separate pamphlet.

Extending the campaign to Scotland

Campaigning work, which had originally been confined to England and Wales, soon spread to Scotland. The Executive Committee agreed that it was important for the name of the Union to become prominent in Scotland too and for a campaign to be held under its auspices. In 1909 the first Scottish anti-vivisection society became affiliated to the Union.

Campaigning in Scotland was found to be of 'a particular arduous nature' because of persistent obstruction by medical students. Edinburgh in particular was regarded as a 'great vivisecting centre' and a campaign shop was opened there. However, on 15 November 1912, the shop at 76 Nicolson Street was stormed and wrecked by students and an ensuing riot led to 26 students being arrested and fined 10s 6d in the Edinburgh police court. It was believed that the main objective of the students had been to seize the experimental instruments displayed in the window.

Miss Grace Hadwen, daughter of Dr Hadwen, and Nurse Cross, the Union's organiser, had been working in the shop at the time and received a brooch from the Union in recognition of their bravery. A letter of thanks was sent to the police officers who had defended the shop and a donation made to the Edinburgh Police Widows and Orphans Fund.

Young supporters of BUAV, 1913

Wrangles over constitutional change

Cobbe had left a substantial sum to the Union in her will but contention over the Constitution of the Union prevented it from receiving her legacy immediately. The sole surviving executor of her will alleged that Union managers had altered one clause in part of the original Constitution: this was deemed to be illegal and meant that the Constitution of the Union did not entitle it to receive the legacy. Miss Kidd reported how the intricacies of the society's Constitution often baffled lawyers and a lengthy legal battle followed. It was not until March 1907, almost three years after Cobbe's death, that the courts ruled that the legacy, minus legal costs, was to be paid to the trustees of the Union

to be applied by them for the general purposes of the British Union for the Abolition of Vivisection in accordance with the Constitution of the said Union.[15]

In view of legal difficulties over the ambiguity in the wording of the Constitution it was decided at the half-yearly meeting of the Board of Managers on 14 May 1908 that

it is most desirable that a new set of rules and regulations for the Constitution of the Union be approved and adopted.[16]

BUAV campaign stall at the Ecclesiastical Art Exhibition, Southampton, 1913

A draft was prepared and sent to all the branches which were asked to appoint a delegate empowered to vote on the matter. A meeting of those delegates took place on 2 July 1908 and the new Constitution was harmoniously adopted after a three-hour discussion. The Union was now more confident that it existed on a sound legal basis. In 1911 all branches were required to adopt a uniform date on which they closed their accounts and these were to be included in the Union's annual report. In its annual report of April 1913 the Union was pleased to be able to report on the 'most cordial relations' between the Union and its numerous branches.

Strengthening the movement: development of a Federation

Because of the increasing size of the Union, both in terms of membership and the number of federated societies, it was felt that there was a need for 'closer co-operation and co-ordination' in order to strengthen the movement. It was therefore proposed to divide the country into convenient divisions and that representatives from the societies in each division would meet no less than twice a year to discuss campaigning methods, arrange meetings and compile lists of competent speakers.

The plan was tested first in the London area. The Federation of London Branches held its first meeting on 20 April 1914 followed by quarterly meetings at the offices of the Union. The principal object of these sessions was to set up propaganda meetings in the London district. Unfortunately, this idea had to be abandoned when the First World War broke out, as many of the branches simply ceased to function.

Political campaigning: building a base of political support

The Union still hoped to pass an abolition Bill through Parliament to make the practice of vivisection illegal and therefore relied heavily on the support of MPs who, it was hoped, would vote in favour of this issue. The Union did not align itself to any political party. A Parliamentary Association had been established as a branch of the Union in order to lobby MPs but had ceded from the Union shortly after the move to London.

A parliamentary fund appeal was held during 1907.

The intention was to raise funds to support anti-vivisection parliamentary candidates who, once elected, would effectively form the nucleus of an anti-vivisection party in the House of Commons. This plan was realised when Mr Chancellor MP, a supporter of the British Union, set up an all-party Parliamentary Anti-Vivisection Committee. This committee, which consisted of approximately 50 MPs, was convened to watch over the interests of the anti-vivisection movement and to give support whenever the issue was raised.

Two general elections were held in 1910 and were seen as great opportunities to raise the anti-vivisection question in the political arena. During both the general elections of 1910 all parliamentary candidates were 'interrogated' by letter about their position on an abolition Bill as the Union was prepared to canvass for those holding anti-vivisection views.

The Union hoped that Dr Hadwen would agree to stand as a candidate in a future election but he declined. He was not overly enthusiastic about the political system, generally viewing politicians as people who only cared about getting votes at election time and who regarded the House of Commons as a 'talking shop'. He was not opposed to lobbying MPs as a campaigning method but did feel that the emphasis ought

A parliamentary news section was introduced into *The Abolitionist* to keep readers abreast of political developments

to be on educating the public, making anti-vivisection a popular movement which MPs would then be more keen to respond to.

In 1911 Mr Chancellor was elected as the Parliamentary Representative of the Union. He asked many questions in the House of Commons on the Union's behalf but generally found that the answers were of an 'evasive and unsatisfactory character'. *The Abolitionist* began a section of parliamentary news to report on these issues.

Conflicting views: 'perfectionist' versus 'lesser measures'

With NAVS having returned to its original restrictionist policy, the anti-vivisection movement had become clearly divided into two camps, with the British Union headed by Dr Hadwen representing the abolitionist or 'perfectionist' stance, and NAVS headed by Coleridge representing the policy of 'lesser measures'.

The British Union refused to deviate from an abolition policy: it felt that attempts at compromise could lead to the serious postponement and possible ultimate defeat of an abolition Bill. Restriction was therefore seen as both a 'danger and a hindrance'. It defended its policy as justifiable in the light of recent abolition campaigns in other areas which had achieved their goals by fighting for basic principles. For example the anti-vaccinationists had triumphed in their fight against compulsory vaccination. A conscientious clause had been introduced to enable parents to make a statutory declaration of objection against vaccination within four months of the birth of their child. William Lloyd Garrison had eventually secured the abolition of slavery in the United States, and Josephine Butler had succeeded, against almost the entire weight of the medical profession, in gaining the repeal of the Contagious Diseases Acts.

The Union addressed the question of why the two societies could not forget their differences and work together towards their common goal. Speaking in July 1909 at the Fourth Triennial International Congress in London, Miss Kidd explained that while abolitionists opposed vivisection as a system, restrictionists proposed on what terms and conditions it should be carried out and this only served to strengthen government protection of vivisection. They maintained that while a restrictionist policy could also support abolition as an ultimate aim, the relationship could not work the other way round as it would be a compromise of principles.

The Union could not forget the betrayal surrounding the 1876 Act and advised delegates from other countries, many of whom did not have legislation in place

never try to run vivisection on your own lines, for you will only be hoodwinked.[17]

The British Union also had a practice of not establishing branches where one already existed for the London Anti-Vivisection Society as long as this society continued to adhere to abolition principles. (LAVS had been founded in 1876 on the principle of total abolition and had agreed to be 'in alliance' with the British Union.) The Union felt it was more important to concentrate on propaganda work where 'no seed had been sown at all' or where 'false principles were being taught'.

A 'great schism' divides the international movement

July 1909 saw a wave of anti-vivisection activity in London as two international congresses were held in the same month. The fact that two congresses were held was also indicative of the differences in policies: one was a restriction congress and one an abolition congress. A 'great schism'[18] had divided the anti-vivisection movement on a global scale and the

cause was being bled to weakness by its self-inflicted wounds.[19]

The restrictionist congress took place between 7 and 10 July 1909 and was organised by Miss Louise Lind-af-Hageby, a Swedish anti-vivisectionist living in England. She had hoped to overcome the question of tactical differences and focus on the common goal - the abolition of vivisection. The abolitionists or 'perfectionists' though were not won over by her plea that there was 'room for everyone' and the British Union issued a warning that any organisation or individual allying themselves to this congress would be expelled from the Union.

The abolitionist congress ran from 19 to 24 July and was organised by the World League Against Vivisection. This was its Fourth Triennial International Congress. The World League had been founded in the

Demonstration in Trafalgar Square following the fourth Triennial Congress of the World League of the Opponents of Vivisection, 24 July, 1909

same year as the British Union by Herr Rudolf Bergner and Miss Kate Deighton. This congress was better documented than the restrictionist congress as it published a full report of its proceedings.

The question of abolition as the only acceptable policy was raised on the first morning. Rule three of the membership of the World League stated that it was open to societies and individuals 'in favour of total abolition of vivisection, and its prohibition by law'. Dr Hadwen, one of the delegates for the British Union, proposed that the words 'without attempts at compromise of any kind' should be added. His resolution was

debated for the rest of the morning. Some societies wanted to be left to implement their principles in their own way, particularly those representing countries without any legislation at all. The amendment was eventually carried and

intolerance was written into the rules.[20]

This congress ended in a procession on 24 July from Hyde Park to Trafalgar Square where the crowds overflowed onto the steps of the National Gallery. The event was seen as a 'brilliant success'.

CHAPTER 4

1881 to 1911

The pro-vivisection response: opposing threats to scientific and medical progress

Cobbe gave recognition to the few who she believed carried out their work with loathing in the 'ardour of scientific research'. She believed they would not only end up repenting what they had done, but that they would denounce the practice completely. Generally, though, she considered vivisection to be a 'heart hardening' practice and vivisectors such as Professor Schiff and Claude Bernard she denounced as 'cruel and callous'.

The brown dog affair

Cobbe had encountered clashes with vivisectors but it was Stephen Coleridge, Honorary Secretary of NAVS, who was to be charged with libel following his attack on a vivisector. In 1903 he publicly accused Dr William Bayliss of breaking the law after reading the manuscript of a diary of two Swedish women, Louise Lind-af-Hageby and Louisa Schartau. These two women were active anti-vivisectionists in their home country but had enrolled at the London School of Medicine for Women in order to gain medical knowledge for themselves so they could argue with vivisectors from an educated standpoint. The course they enrolled on gave them the right to attend courses on physiology, including demonstrations, at three other London universities.

They attended these demonstrations and kept a diary of all their observations which they later published as *The Shambles of Science*. One chapter in the first edition they entitled 'Fun' and in it described a demonstration they had witnessed at University College, London, where a dog with a recent abdominal wound

Claude Bernard - 'the prince of vivisectors'

Courtesy of Mary Evans Picture Library

struggled throughout the demonstration. Coleridge, having some knowledge of the law, immediately saw two breaches of the law in their account as no animal could be used for more than one experiment and any animal used for a lecture demonstration had to be fully anaesthetised.

The provisions of the 1876 Act only gave six months for contraventions to be brought to the attention of the Home Secretary. With little time to spare, Coleridge instead made a public accusation against Bayliss knowing that if he did not respond it would be as good as admitting the charge, and if he sued him for libel it would at least bring the matter to court, thus gaining the desired publicity.

In the event Bayliss did sue Coleridge for libel, and a court case followed. Although it was concluded in court that the evidence was inconclusive, the matter had been brought to the attention of the public and was widely reported in the press. Coleridge was ordered to pay Bayliss £2,000 in damages but an appeal fund by *The Daily News* soon raised more than this amount leaving NAVS with a surplus of several hundred pounds.

At the instigation of Louisa Woodward, Honorary Secretary of the Society for United Prayer for the Prevention of Cruelty to Animals, a drinking fountain was erected in Latchmere Recreation Ground, in London's Battersea, as a memorial to the brown dog. The money for the memorial was raised by public subscription and was unveiled by the Mayor of Battersea in September 1906. The statue bore the inscription

In memory of the brown terrier dog done to death in the laboratories of University College in February 1903, after having endured vivisection extending over more than two months and having been handed from one vivisector to another till death came to his release.
Also in memory of the 232 dogs vivisected at the same place during the year 1902. Men and women of England, how long shall these things be?[21]

In 1907 the statue was attacked by medical students from University College who felt that their college had been singled out unfairly for criticism. They did not, however, succeed in their attempt to destroy the statue which was placed under police protection. The medical students held demonstrations and disrupted anti-vivisection meetings. There were numerous arrests over the following months. The police bore the financial burden of maintaining a 24-hour watch over what had become a highly contentious statue. The local council refused a request from the police to take it down: the people of Battersea were determined to keep 'our dorg'.

In 1910 however the newly elected Battersea borough council decided that the monument should be removed. Mr Fraser Hewes, Honorary Secretary of the Nottingham branch of the Union, wrote to the council making an offer for the brown dog statue which he wanted to put in his garden alongside his already well-known anti-vivisection advertising board. But the statue was removed secretly in the dead of night and is said to have been handed over to a blacksmith to be melted down.

The statue and the public interest it aroused gained enormous publicity for the anti-vivisection movement and the British Union recorded in its annual report for 1908 that the previous year had witnessed a remarkable awakening of interest in the anti-vivisection cause. The case of the brown dog must certainly have been a contributory factor.

In 1985 a new brown dog statue, funded by BUAV and NAVS, was unveiled in Battersea Park. The bronze statue, sculpted by Nicola Hicks, was only accepted by the Greater London Council on condition that it had libel insurance to cover the wording of the inscription, which was the same as on the original statue. Although the *British Medical Journal* denounced the memorial as

RCHME © Crown Copyright

The original brown dog statue with its controversial inscription was unveiled in Latchmere Recreation Ground, Battersea, in 1906 and led to the brown dog riots of the following year

Medical students rioted and attempted to destroy the brown dog statue, 1907

The new brown dog statue which stands today in Battersea Park, erected in 1985

'degrading, libellous and offensive', the statue has never attracted the same degree of controversy as the original statue which had been attacked with sledgehammers and crowbars.

Early defence: response to anti-vivisection agitation

The development of an anti-vivisection movement had instilled in the vivisectors a need for some kind of self-protection. The Physiological Society of Great Britain was established in response to anti-vivisection agitation, and it complained to the Home Office that the 1876 Act would be a hindrance to its research. In 1881, at the International Medical Congress in London, a resolution was passed recognising the value of experiments on animals and that it was not desirable to restrict 'competent persons' in this practice. The anti-vivisectionists however scrutinised the debates of the Congress for any contraventions of the Act which led to the prosecution of a Professor Ferrier for an alleged infringement. His subsequent acquittal served to infuriate both the anti-vivisectionists (who regarded the Act as futile) and the vivisectors (who saw the need for some form of protection from continual harassment).

Anti-vivisectionists were regarded by their opponents as a hindrance to the progress of science and medicine, and a threat to their tenuous social status. Medical men had worked hard throughout the 19th century to raise the status of their profession. They had made considerable progress, and were not prepared to see this effort reversed. The causes of scientific progress and pro-vivisection had become firmly linked.

In 1882 the Association for the Advancement of Medicine by Research (AAMR) was formed to educate the public about the value of experimental medicine. In fact, the Association was no more than a society of vivisectors whose aim was the repeal, or at least the modification, of the 1876 Act. The organisation took on a self-appointed role as adviser to the Home Office where they appeared to 'rule the roost' on issuing licences, registration of premises and other workings of the Act. While not a secret relationship, it was not exactly publicised, and the anti-vivisectionists were dismayed to learn that the pro-vivisectionists seemed to 'have found a back entrance to the corridors of power'.[22]

They argued that this had allowed a massive increase in the number of experiments to take place, which was duly reflected in the Home Office annual returns. In 1882, when AAMR was established, there were 481 experiments recorded by the Home Office. By 1900 this had reached a massive 10,839.

Stephen Coleridge, Honorary Secretary of NAVS, spoke out against this relationship, which had no legal basis, in his evidence to the second Royal Commission on vivisection. He accused the Home Office of

having placed themselves in improper confidential relations with a private society composed of supporters of vivisection.[23]

Vivisectionists' self-preservation and their 'cloak of caution'

Although the AAMR had defined its objective as the education of the public, this work did not really begin until the Research Defence Society (RDS) was established in 1908 by Stephen Paget. Paget, the son of an eminent surgeon, had been Secretary of AAMR for the previous 12 years and was regarded by the British Union as

the chosen champion of the whole army of working vivisectors.[24]

The object of the Research Defence Society was to

make generally known as to experiments on animals in this country and the regulations under which they are conducted, the immense importance of such experiments to the welfare of mankind, and the great saving of human and animal life and health which is already due to them.[25]

The British Union regarded the establishment of such an organisation as 'proof of the success of our efforts'. It felt that its activities were not only resented by vivisectors, but regarded as a genuine threat. The Union took it as a compliment that it was worthy of such attention. For every pamphlet issued by the RDS, a 'counterblast' would be issued by the Union.

As well as forming organisations to protect their interests, vivisectors in Britain also learnt quickly to adopt a cautious style in the presentation of their work. This was because anti-vivisectionists were constantly monitoring the scientific press for exposure of cruelty inadvertently admitted when scientists wrote up their experiments. This self-preservation, alluded to as a 'cloak of caution', contrasted greatly with the 'engaged frankness' of the continental vivisectors of the late 19th century. Vivisectors in Britain were exposed to 'a much more active and highly organised criticism than exists on the continent'[26] and they therefore learnt quickly the art of concealment and would take precautions when writing accounts of their work for a British scientific journal.

The anti-vivisectionists were also conscious of their own style of presentation and the British Union was keen to be seen as attacking the *practice* of vivisection and not its practitioners. Although it disliked vivisectors, the Union resisted the temptation to attack them on a personal level and reserved 'their adjectives for the deed rather than the doer'.[27]

Reactions to the second Royal Commission: highlighting tactical differences

In December 1906 the government appointed a second Royal Commission on vivisection to examine the workings of the Act which had now been in existence for 30 years. The British Union was very sceptical about the Commission and considered it an attempt by government to shelve the issue and to avoid facing questions raised by the recent presentation of an abolition Bill in Parliament.

From the outset it expected the results of the Commission to be a 'foregone conclusion' from which some 'unmeaning and unsatisfactory compromise will be attempted'. The Union was reluctant to place any confidence in the Commission and had concerns about its constitution and procedures as the sittings of the Com-

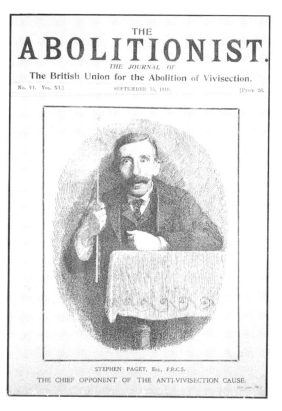

THE
ABOLITIONIST.
THE JOURNAL OF
The British Union for the Abolition of Vivisection.
No. VI. Vol. XI.]   SEPTEMBER 15, 1910.   [Price 2d.

STEPHEN PAGET, Esq., F.R.C.S.
THE CHIEF OPPONENT OF THE ANTI-VIVISECTION CAUSE.

Stephen Paget, who founded the Research Defence Society in 1908, as depicted on the cover of *The Abolitionist,* **15 September 1910**

Lady Kathleen Bushe and Lady Tenterden campaigning against the National Insurance Bill, 28 October 1911

mission were to be held in secret.

The British Union proposed that Dr Hadwen should sit on the Commission. This was rejected on the grounds that he was too deeply committed to opposition, which meant that no medical representative from the anti-vivisection movement was invited to join the Commission. On the other hand, the pro-vivisection voice was clearly represented. Of the five medical men on the Commission, three were, or had been, licensed vivisectors and one was a 'pronounced supporter' of vivisection. The British Union could not forget the 'disastrous results' of the first Royal Commission. It therefore felt reluctant to waste time assisting with a further Royal Commission which was not going to reach an impartial view. It therefore passed a resolution refusing to submit evidence.

The reaction to the second Royal Commission again highlighted differences in the tactics of the anti-vivisection movement. Whereas the British Union had effectively boycotted the Commission, Coleridge and Lind-af-Hageby both gave evidence. Coleridge listed a string of accusations against the Home Office in his three-day evidence which was published as a separate book by his society.

All the proceedings of the Commission were published verbatim but the British Union argued that few people would be able to afford to buy these, let alone have time to wade through and read them. One keen follower of these minutes was George Bernard Shaw, who published his play *A Doctor's Dilemma* in 1906. The Union felt that his discussion of the matter in the play's preface added a 'brilliant and forcible plea' to the debate.

The Commission's final report did not appear until 12 March 1912, by which time three of its members, including its Chairman, had died. It had taken six years to reach its conclusion in contrast to the six months of the first Commission in 1875. However, the final report was not unanimous. While a majority thought that no further legislation was necessary, a minority took the opposite view. The final outcome did not lead to new legislation but some changes were made to the administration of the Act. The British Union had never expected any legislative change to result from the Commission as this would have meant discussing the issue in Parliament.

A new advisory body was to be set up to replace the role of AAMR. However, as the Home Secretary asked

The great anti-vivisection demonstration from The Embankment to Hyde Park protesting against the National Insurance Bill, 28 October 1911

for the assistance of the Royal College of Physicians and the Royal College of Surgeons to appoint this body, the British Union felt

the difference between the new body and the old will be the difference between Tweedledum and Tweedledee.[28]

The final report included a Reservation Memorandum issued by Dr George Wilson, one of the Commissioners. While he had deliberately not allied himself to any anti-vivisection society, he was clearly sympathetic to the cause and felt an 'abiding sense of duty and responsibility' to explain his inability to endorse all the opinions of his colleagues.

National Insurance Bill: publicly subsidised cruelty

The primary purpose of the National Insurance Bill of 1911 was to provide workers with insurance and protection against unemployment, sickness and disability. However it was actively opposed by the anti-vivisectionists because of clause 15, section B, which set aside £62,500 a year for research. The anti-vivisectionists, for whom research had become synonymous with experimentation on animals, felt that this government funding was tantamount to the 'state endowment of vivisection' and that making money available for research would actually serve only as an incentive to the practice.

This proposed research endowment was a serious

This bust of Queen Victoria, who declared vivisection to be 'a disgrace to Christianity and humanity', was the 'pièce de résistance' in the demonstration against the National Insurance Bill, 28 October 1911

blow to the anti-vivisection cause and was one of the few occasions when anti-vivisectionists wanted to be seen as a coherent movement. Societies right across the board came together to represent the current anti-vivisection feeling in the country. Headed by Mr Chancellor, the Parliamentary Representative of the British Union, they arranged a deputation to meet the Chancellor of the Exchequer, Mr Lloyd George, on 1 August 1911 to express their concerns. However Mr George was tied up in business at the House and had to send a representative to meet the deputation on his behalf instead.

On Saturday 28 October 1911, an anti-vivisection demonstration against clause 15, section B was organised by the British Union. This was regarded as the most important day that year. The procession marched from The Embankment to Hyde Park fronted by a banner which simply said 'No Vivisection'. Other campaigning banners followed, predominantly in red and white, the recently adopted colours of the Union. The 'pièce de resistance' of the procession was a carriage whose sole occupant was a bust of Queen Victoria

who was known to have held strong anti-vivisection views.

In addition to the demonstration the British Union also organised a 'monster petition' of 74,704 signatures which was presented to the House of Commons by Mr Chancellor in November 1911. The campaign however failed its immediate objective as the Bill was passed and became the National Insurance Act of 1911.

The Medical Research Committee, later renamed the Medical Research Council (MRC), was established in 1913 to advise on how the money set aside by Parliament under the National Insurance Act should be spent. Anti-vivisectionists had hoped that living animals would be excluded but were disappointed to learn that any research would be undertaken in accordance with the 1876 Act. The Union objected that this large sum of money would be raised through tax-payers' contributions and that those opposed to vivisection would be compelled to pay for a practice which 'violated their consciences'. Cruelty subsidised by public funds constituted the 'rankest injustice'.

CHAPTER 5

The first world war years

The war years - and the Union's 'unpatriotic agitation'

During the First World War the campaigning activities of the Union went through an inevitable lull as the nation became preoccupied with the war effort. Open air meetings were greatly reduced and the shop campaigns, which had become an essential campaigning technique, went into abeyance. While many of the branches put their activities on hold altogether and reported a reduction in membership, the work of headquarters was less affected and during these years it focused almost exclusively on the anti-vaccination issue.

Campaigning against the government was not easy during the war. The British Union was threatened with prosecution under the Defence of the Realm Acts, cited in the House of Commons for 'unpatriotic agitation', denounced by MPs for the spread of 'pernicious literature' and boycotted by the press because of government censorship. Despite these restrictions the Union still managed to achieve a great deal, particularly in alerting soldiers to the fact that it was their liberty to refuse vaccinations if they wished.

The Union did initiate some new campaigning techniques in this period. Large posters were placed in fields just outside London and could be seen by train passengers as they approached the city. And as the number of meetings declined sharply, *The Abolitionist* became even more important as a channel of communication.

Union opposition to compulsory vaccination

The British Union was opposed to compulsory vaccination and its President Dr Hadwen was well known for his views on the issue. Dr Hadwen had been the first anti-vaccinationist to be summoned in the County of Somerset following the birth of his eldest child Una in 1879. The law demanded that she should be vaccinated but after hearing about some 'horrible cases of dis-

ease' resulting from vaccination, he made his own thorough study of anti-vaccination literature resolving 'that the lancet of the vaccinator should never touch his child's arm'.[29] His refusal to vaccinate Una brought him before the magistrates' bench four times and cost him £50. He was also brought before the bench three times for his son John, and twice for his second daughter Grace, before they finally gave him up 'as a bad job!'.

Dr Hadwen had defended his right to protect his own children against the possible side-effects resulting from vaccination and felt that all parents should be entitled to do the same. He was chiefly instrumental in bringing about the introduction of a conscientious clause in 1907, when parents were finally given a choice over whether or not to vaccinate their children.

The British Union's campaign against vaccination was based on both the moral and the scientific arguments. Huge numbers of animals were being used in vaccination experiments, which was clearly evident from the annual Home Office statistics, and these animals suffered a great deal more than just receiving a

BUAV tried to expose the cruelty behind vaccination research

'pin-prick' as was suggested. The Union saw how the development of vaccines had brought about a new type of vivisection with animals being injected with 'noxious substances'. It was further argued that vaccination was a scientifically flawed method which was both dangerous in application and uncertain in results, leading to a number of side-effects and even death to those receiving vaccinations.

Soldiers recruited into the army during the First World War were expected to receive a number of vaccinations. The British Union took up their cause so that soldiers could choose whether or not to be vaccinated. Soldiers who had refused to be vaccinated had been discriminated against and, as a punishment, refused their leave. The Union succeeded in getting confirmation from Parliament that vaccination was, indeed, voluntary and that soldiers would not be punished for refusing vaccinations. Mr Chancellor, the Parliamentary Representative of the British Union, obtained a statement from Lord Kitchener, the Secretary for War, stating that 'no pressure was to be brought to bear' on objectors. The War Office issued a statement to commanding officers stating that uninoculated men should not be refused their leave.

The Union invested a large amount of resources in publicising this information and raising awareness among new conscripts of their rights. Whole page advertisements were taken out in the leading London and provincial newspapers, leaflets were distributed to soldiers by hand and copies were also sent to their mess rooms. *The Abolitionist* was sent to the army officers and to their doctors' quarters. 'Our Soldier Friends' became a regular feature in *The Abolitionist* during the war years.

The Union took up the cases of individual soldiers who had been refused their rights and a fund was established to help initiate legal proceedings on their behalf. The whole campaign was a considerable expense but the Union felt it was worthwhile in light of government threats to make vaccination compulsory again.

The League of Nations: maintaining peace or endowing vivisection?

The League of Nations was an international alliance for the preservation of peace, established in 1920 shortly after the end of the First World War. The British Union

BUAV backed the National Canine Defence League's demand for the exemption of dogs from vivisection

Courtesy of Mary Evans Picture Library

was opposed to the fact that the Health Section of the League allied itself with the acceptance of 'modern medicine'. This included the use of vaccines which had been developed by means of vivisection.

The branches, as well as the headquarters, of the Union repeatedly forwarded resolutions to the Secretary of the League protesting against its Health Section policy. But the Secretary clearly had no sympathy for the anti-vivisection cause though his comment that the British Union 'seems to be a well organised society, and is stirring up its branches and members, so that we receive some kind of anti-vivisection protest almost every day'[30] did at least provide some amusement at the Union's annual council meeting of branch delegates in 1922.

The Union regretted the League's decision to com-

Supporters of the Dogs (Protection) Bill, 1919

Courtesy of Mary Evans Picture Library

Strays from homes for lost dogs were trained for service in the First World War – a retrieved helmet was an indication of a wounded soldier in need of help

mission further experiments to standardise serums and vaccines. It argued that serum and vaccine treatments not only involved cruelty to animals, but also represented an unnecessary danger to humans and had a long record of failure. It felt that the League should confine itself to 'sanitary and hygienic' measures of dealing with disease.

The Union's feeling was that the primary purpose of the League, which was the preservation of peace, had been overshadowed by its involvement with vivisection. In its campaign against the League, the British Union asked was it formed for the maintenance of peace or for the endowment of vivisection?

Dogs: a stepping stone to 'fight for the rest of creation'

Many people thought that animals such as dogs and cats should be exempt from vivisection. Richard Hult Hutton of the first Royal Commission had argued that these species should be granted exemption on the grounds of their special relationship with mankind, their higher sensibility, the criminal trade by which they were supplied to laboratories and the absence of any proof of their indispensability to science. The issue was addressed again by the second Royal Commission, but members had found 'some difficulty in deciding upon this important question'[31] and no action was taken.

Dogs had been afforded some protection from vivisection under the Dogs Act 1906 which made it illegal to give or sell stray dogs to laboratories. Earlier than this a parliamentary Bill had been drafted to exempt dogs from vivisection altogether. The Dogs (Protection)

Bill was first introduced in 1903; after 1908 it became the work of Sir Frederick Banbury who swore that the Bill would be introduced in every session until it was passed.

Campaigning for this Bill was largely the work of the National Canine Defence League (NCDL) and the British Union saw the Bill as belonging to the League. However the Union was willing to lend its support as the Bill was calling for the abolition of a certain category of vivisection - not just its restriction. Although the Union did not wish to be seen to be campaigning for the exclusion of just one species, it nevertheless felt that the Bill should not be opposed. It did, after all, embrace the notion of the abolition of vivisection, even if only applied to dogs. The Union agreed that if the Bill was successful, the exemption of dogs should be used as a stepping stone to go on and 'fight for the rest of creation'. In 1914 passage of the Bill had looked hopeful when it reached a second reading in the House of Commons, but it was wrecked at the committee stage and, following the outbreak of war, all controversial legislation was vetoed.

Dogs at war

Dogs were drafted into the war effort by all sides in their thousands to serve as 'mercy dogs'. Ambulance dogs could be used to seek out wounded men, and carry a small pack of medical supplies and flasks of water or spirits in saddlebags. They were trained to retrieve the helmet or a piece of clothing from a wounded soldier as evidence of a man in need of help,

BUAV and NCDL held a demonstration in Parliament Square while the Dogs (Protection) Bill was debated in Parliament, 23 May 1919

or they would simply provide a last moment of companionship to a dying soldier. The larger dogs were able to drag men to safety and to pull small ambulance carts. Messenger dogs were used to relay messages in small canisters attached to their collars when all other lines of communication had broken down.

The Abolitionist recounts the story of how the officer of a soldier left badly wounded between enemy lines tied a note to a dog's collar asking the Germans if their man could be recovered. The dog returned with a reply stating that they had five minutes to do so - and the man was rescued. A cheer for the enemy was heard by way of thanks before normal business was resumed.[32]

When the war was over, women were enfranchised under the Representation of the People Act 1918, largely for their work in the war. But the work of the dogs was not to be so gratefully acknowledged. The Dogs (Protection) Bill came very close to becoming legislation in 1919 but, again, was stopped. Although the issue rumbled on well into the 1920s, dogs were never granted their exemption.

The British Union was not surprised by the legislative failure and echoed the words of its founder, Frances Power Cobbe, who had said that it was useless to appeal to Parliament until the public had been fully instructed. The Union felt that public opinion was 'not yet ripe'.

CHAPTER 6

The 1920s

Spreading the word: the Union extends its influence at home and abroad

During the war years many branches had cut back their activities or stagnated altogether, but after the war they began to rejuvenate their campaigning work. The size and activities of the branches varied quite significantly and some took longer than others to re-establish themselves. The anti-vivisection movement in general is thought to have stagnated after the First World War as 'survivors turned their attention to the welfare of their own species'[33] but by the end of the 1920s the Union had reached unprecedented growth with a record num-ber of members and branches. The first overseas branches were established in this period. By the end of the 1920s the British Union had over 150 branches worldwide and was, without doubt, the largest society of its kind in the world.

New campaigning techniques were also necessary in this new era. Van campaigns were to become an essential method of spreading the anti-vivisection message at home, while Dr Hadwen promoted the cause overseas when he undertook a lecture tour of the United States.

Re-establishment and growth of the branches

Some of the smaller branches had less than 10 members while the largest numbered over 1,000. Nottingham and Manchester had always been two of the largest and most active branches but, within just three years, they were equalled by the recently established branch in Melbourne, Australia. Regular meetings were held again and the shop campaigns, which had been postponed during the war, were re-established.

It was at this time that the idea of forming regional federations was taken up again. As the size and finances of the branches varied so considerably, they began to establish federations in order to share resources. The Southern Federation was the first to be set up and this was for the purpose of buying a van to visit the smaller towns and villages which the shop campaigns had not reached. The van campaign was run by Union organiser Maurice Toms, and the first touring campaign took place in May 1924. The campaign was a success and the technique was recommended to other branches. Soon, other federations started to form so that they too could run van campaigns. Headquarters also became involved and by 1929 the Union had six vans at its disposal. These were all the same colour and therefore recognisable as 'the anti-vivisection vans'.

The vans were described as 'shops on wheels'.

BUAV campaign poster 1920's

Cartoon of the first BUAV anti-vivisection van, 1924

They had fold-down side flaps which were used to display literature and to exhibit model animals and vivisection instruments.

Funds from the public purse: a 'monstrous imposition'

The campaign against the use of public money to fund vivisection was taken up again after the First World War, and rekindled the debate over the 'state endowment of vivisection'. The Medical Research Committee, which had been established in 1913 to decide how the funds should be spent, was incorporated by Royal Charter in 1920 and renamed the Medical Research Council. As its funds came from a grant from the national Exchequer, to which the ordinary tax-payer contributed, members of the public had no choice about whether or not their money went to fund animal experiments. County councils and municipal corporations which had their own laboratories also depended on rate-payers' money to fund them. This expenditure, argued the Union, represented a 'monstrous imposition upon the public purse'.

The British Union also argued that the Medical Research Council had in fact more money than it knew what to do with. It regularly gave examples of experiments carried out with the use of such money which it condemned as unscientific and 'devised' purely for the purposes of spending the large amount of money available for research. The Union argued that during Lloyd George's administration 'the medicine men had the time of their lives'[34] as vivisection had become one of the richest endowed institutions of the state.

Since its establishment, the British Union had devoted a lot of energy into making the general public aware

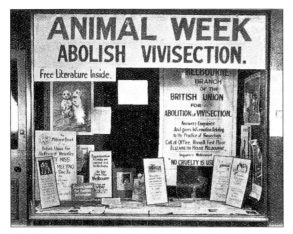

The first Australian branch of BUAV was established in Melbourne in 1923

Protesters in Hampstead during Animal Welfare Week, May 1928

of the existence of vivisection. It now tried to make them aware that they were 'being fleeced of their money for the purpose of upholding and perpetuating it'.[35]

It also argued that

no nation or government has any right to force upon us the responsibility for a practice against which we protest.[36]

The Union promoted a Bill 'to prevent the application of public money to vivisection experiments'. This was introduced into the House of Commons three times: in 1922, 1924 and 1930. The first time it was introduced, on 10 May 1922, it constituted a strike at the financial side of the business. Lieutenant-Commander Kenworthy, who introduced the Bill, argued for support purely on economic grounds, not on the merits or demerits of vivisection.

However, the Bill failed, as it did on both its second and third attempts, and never became law.

Dr Hadwen visits the United States

Dr Hadwen made two visits to the United States during the 1920s. He was initially invited by the President of the Californian Anti-Vivisection Society, Mrs Rosamond Rae Wright, to 'come over and help us'. The State of California was due to hold a referendum and one of the

Tea in the garden after the demonstration in Hampstead, May 1928

issues to be voted on was the abolition of vivisection. Dr Hadwen also had a personal desire to visit the United States as he wished to visit the grave of his son John who had died during the war and was buried in San Diego, California.

Hadwen sailed from Southampton on 1 May 1921 and was met off the boat in New York one week later by Mrs Diana Belais, President of the New York Anti-Vivisection Society. A public luncheon was held in his honour. There he was able to meet many of his Ameri-

A new Southern Federation van, 1926

The Western Federation van, 1926

can friends in the cause until then only known to him by name. Although he had come with the intention of visiting California he took the opportunity to visit many other cities to spread the anti-vivisection word.

He visited Boston, Philadelphia and Washington before returning to New York for an anti-vivisection Interstate Conference which was attended by about 30 different societies. He then visited several cities in the western states before returning to Washington where he gave evidence before the Senate Committee. The Senate was considering a Bill to prohibit the use of dogs in vivisection, an issue that was also very much alive at home, and Hadwen was invited to give evidence to the sub-committee appointed to consider the Bill. He was also invited to the White House to meet President Harding.

Dr Hadwen returned to England on 12 July 1921 to find that his visit had provoked a storm of protest from the pro-vivisection lobby in the United States. A society similar to the Research Defence Society had been established. It produced a number of publications in which numerous personal attacks on Dr Hadwen were made, the tone of which was far more 'vulgar' than anything published by even his most firmly established enemies in Britain. The effect of his visit to the United States was clearly evident.

The referendum in the State of California had been unsuccessful with the proposal to abolish vivisection voted down. Hadwen remained undeterred, however, and returned in September 1922 to campaign again on the issue. He undertook an extensive tour covering some 30,000 miles and was lecturing or debating practically every day.

A centenary of animal rights

The year 1922 saw the passing of 100 years since Martin's Act had come into effect. The British Union celebrated this event as the Act had introduced the principle of the rights of animals into legislation for the first time. It also had a 'valuable train of consequences' as other acts followed which prohibited the deliberate infliction of suffering on animals.

The last week of May 1922 was dedicated to celebrating the Act, starting with Sunday 21 May when clergy were asked to preach on the subject. Teachers were encouraged to address the question of humanity in schools all week, branches of the Union held meetings, and a public meeting was planned for Friday 26 May in Queens Hall, followed by a procession and demonstration in Hyde Park on the following day.

The public meeting to celebrate Martin's Act took the place of the Union's usual annual public meeting. All members were encouraged to attend and to try to bring at least six friends along. The meeting was an obvious success. The Hall was packed 'from floor to ceiling' and it was claimed that 'never before has so large an audience listened in London to an anti-vivisection speech'.[37]

While the Union was celebrating the introduction of animal rights into legislation, it remained fully aware that laboratory animals had not been accorded the same legislative rights. It vowed to keep fighting until this flaw in legislation had been removed.

The Union proves a trade in stolen dogs

The campaign for the exemption of dogs from vivisection carried on into the 1920s. Vivisectors often claimed that dogs were difficult to obtain for research purposes:

in addition, the Dogs Act 1906 had prohibited stray dogs being 'given or sold for the purposes of vivisection'. However, according to the Home Office annual returns, hundreds of dogs were being used each year in experiments. Purpose-bred laboratory dogs did not exist then, so the question had to be asked: 'Where did all these dogs come from?'

The British Union was able to prove that a definite trade in stolen dogs existed and that at least one laboratory in London had been the receiver of these stolen goods. In 1926, two cases of dog stealing brought the issue into the national press and the pro-vivisection lobby had to defend its use of dogs in medical research rigorously.

The first case was that of Henry William Hewitt who was charged at Bow Street police court on 20 November 1926 with stealing two Irish terrier puppies from outside a shop off London's Tottenham Court Road. Hewitt was caught red-handed by RSPCA Inspector Curley while carrying the dogs in a sack.

It transpired that Hewitt was employed by the School of Physiology at the University College of London to supply dogs for experimental purposes for six shillings each. In his defence, Professor C Lovatt Evans said that he had purchased the dogs believing them to be legally obtained. Hewitt, who was already known to have supplied cats to laboratories, and had previously been convicted of dog stealing, was sentenced to six months' hard labour for stealing the dogs and a further month of imprisonment for cruelty.

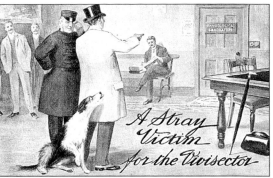

Courtesy of Mary Evans Picture Library

Scientists argued that stray dogs should be handed over to laboratories for experiments

Questions about the case were asked in the House of Commons. Dr Salter MP suggested that the Home Secretary should make arrangements to allocate for scientific purposes some of the 50,000 stray dogs destroyed each year. A letter in *The Times* (26 November 1926) from the former distinguished University College physiologist AV Hill also suggested that these unwanted dogs should be used for experimental purposes.

The British Union held poster parades twice a day for two weeks. On 25 November 1926 a letter of protest was handed in to the School of Physiology by Mrs Keith Mackenzie, a member of the Executive Committee of the British Union. She requested an interview and permission to inspect the laboratories but this, not surprisingly, was refused.

Meanwhile, on 19 November 1926, a wolfhound mongrel called Bob had been taken from his home at 35 Doughty Street. His owner, Frederick Smythe, had informed the police and visited the local dogs home but without any success. After reading about the case of Hewitt in the newspaper he went to University College on 22 November to see if the same fate had happened to Bob.

Mr Smythe met Professor Verney at the University and gave him Bob's description. After checking the kennels, Professor Verney told Smythe that nothing could be done without first consulting the Provost and he was told to return the next day. On his return Mr Smythe was reunited with Bob. He hadn't escaped without injury though and a large lump on the base of his skull suggested a blow to the head. The British

Polly and Molly, the two rescued Irish terriers

Mrs Keith Mackenzie tries to gain entrance to University College, London, following the revelation that the School of Physiology had received stolen dogs, 25 November 1926

Union provided legal help and financial assistance for the case, and Mr Smythe and Bob became Union celebrities. Their appearance at a public meeting on 19 January 1927 was 'greeted with much applause'.

George Phipps was charged on 22 December 1926 at Clerkenwell police court with the theft of Bob, but was acquitted. The Union also took the 'bold step' of prosecuting Professor Verney for being in possession of the dog 'knowing it to be stolen'. Verney was acquitted on a technical point because legal possession could not be traced to him. The outcome was what the Union had expected but it had achieved much in the way of publicity. The issue of the use of dogs in medical research was reported in national newspapers and in the medical journals.

The British Union highlighted these cases as reasons why the public should demand the abolition, and not the regulation, of vivisection. It argued that no-one owning a pet could feel secure as long as this exploitation of domestic animals was allowed.

Nothing but the prohibition of vivisection can stop this nefarious trade.[38]

The Dogs (Protection) Bill fails again

The following year the Dogs (Protection) Bill was presented yet again - on 14 February 1927 - and, for the first time, it was also supported by the RSPCA. The pro-vivisection lobby leapt to the defence of the use of dogs in medical research and the activities of the RSPCA and NCDL in lobbying for support of the Bill were attacked by the pro-vivisectionists as a 'serious annoyance by crank societies'.[39]

The RDS published an article in its journal on the importance of dogs in medical research and deplored the RSPCA's decision to support the Bill. The RDS also thought it notable that Mr Fry, the magistrate in Hewitt's case, had said in conclusion: 'Anything I can do to stop this sort of thing I will' and reported in its journal that the magistrate had given 'vent to an expression of opinion which savoured of anti-vivisection sentiment'.

The Science Committee of the British Medical Association prepared a memorandum setting out why dogs were essential to certain classes of experiments. It argued that dogs were physiologically similar to man and healthy monkeys were difficult to obtain in large quantities. It highlighted the use of dogs by Banting and Best, who were credited with the discovery of insulin, and argued that the exemption of dogs would kill the progress of medical science. It organised a major conference in April 1927 to discuss the issue, which attracted some of the leading figures in British medicine including Lord Dawson, the King's physician.

Physician Thomas Lewis, who had been a student of the notorious Victor Horsley, also entered into the debate as he had used dogs in his electrocardiograph work. He wrote to the BMA urging the medical profession to organise a petition stating that the use of dogs was necessary for the progress of medical science. He also urged that such a petition should state that stray dogs should be allowed to be used for vivisection purposes. In addition, he wrote to the editor of the *British Medical Journal* expressing concern over the 'large amount of hearsay that has fallen into the lap of the enemy'[40], and attacked the NCDL petition for its accusation that dogs were used in agonising experiments. Finally, Lewis went on to defend University College as a 'premier centre of medical research' and attacked the anti-vivisectionists as a 'curious group'.

Medical lobbying achieved its objective and, once more, the Dogs (Protection) Bill was lost. Later the Medical Research Council published a memorandum on the Bill defending the practice of using dogs, repudiating accusations of torture and recommending that stray dogs be made available for experimentation.

Political disappointment

In June 1929 a new Labour government was elected under Ramsay MacDonald. MacDonald, along with his Home Secretary JR Clynes and two other ministers, Philip Snowden and Arthur Henderson, were known to be opposed to vivisection and had all been vice presidents of Louise Lind-af-Hageby's international congress in July 1909.

It was therefore not unnatural that those who had the cause at heart were expectant.[41]

A letter from the Home Secretary was to bring early disappointment to those who were anticipating political reform. It read

I doubt whether any Minister could ever undertake public responsibilities in a Department covering a great variety of work, if in all respects he had to harmonise his public duties with his private opinion.[42]

Clynes had not altered his private opinion on vivisection. But when yet another attempt was made to obtain the exemption of dogs from vivisection he said he would not bring in legislation on this matter. He added that the previous government in 1927 had been advised against it by the Medical Research Council. He stated that it was the duty of the government to be guided by the 'best possible advice'. The names of Mr Clynes and Ramsay MacDonald were eventually removed from the list of the Union's supporters in the House.

Beatrice Kidd retires

One individual who had played an important role in the growth and influence of the society was its Secretary, Miss Kidd. In 1928 she retired from the position which she had held since the Union moved its headquarters to London. In addition to her secretarial duties, Beatrice Kidd (who had begun as the Organising Secretary in 1904) had also acted as a writer, translator, lecturer and debater for the society. On her retirement she accept-

Mr Smythe with Bob, who was found at University College, London

ed the position of Honorary Secretary so that she could retain some connection with the organisation to which she had devoted 24 years of service.

The British Union: company incorporation

When the Companies Act was passed in 1929, the British Union became incorporated as a company. This gave it a number of legal advantages, in particular about receiving legacies from abroad and by removing individual committee members from liability, for example in the case of a libel trial. The Union was incorporated in November 1929 and the necessary Memorandum and Articles of Association were published.

CHAPTER 7

1923 and 1924

Dr Hadwen on trial (inside and outside court)

One of the most memorable events in the history of the British Union was, perhaps, the charge against Dr Hadwen, President of the Union, of manslaughter in 1924. The charge followed the death of a 10-year-old girl, Nellie Burnham, who had been treated for tonsillitis by Dr Hadwen.

In view of the seriousness of the charge against him, Dr Hadwen immediately offered to resign the presidency of the Union but his offer was not accepted. He was overwhelmed by the amount of letters of sympathy from his supporters, and the committees of Union branches up and down the country passed resolutions expressing messages of sympathy and trust.

The case was heard at the Court of Assizes, Gloucester, between 27 and 29 October 1924. It was alleged that Nellie had died of diphtheria, followed by pneumonia, and that he had failed to diagnose the case of diphtheria and administer the 'proper treatment'. Hadwen however argued that she had had a case of ulcerative tonsillitis and had contracted pneumonia independently through exposure to a chill after the tonsillitis was practically cured.

Dr Hadwen: proponents and opponents

Dr Hadwen, although a practising GP, disagreed strongly with conventional medical thought and was disliked within the medical profession for his dissenting views. As a medical student he had been indoctrinated with the belief that animal experiments were necessary for the benefit of human health, but later decided to

Dr Hadwen

research the matter for himself. He concluded that, aside from moral issues, vivisection was an unsound scientific practice. He was also opposed to the practice of vaccination and had become notorious during the Gloucester smallpox epidemic of 1896 when he claimed that it was in fact unsanitary conditions, not a lack of vaccination, that led to the outbreak of the disease. His campaigns led to improvements in the water supply and the appreciative citizens invited him to set up a practice there.

In the summer of 1896 he bought a house in Brunswick Square, Gloucester, which was to be his home for the rest of his life, and he set up a medical practice. For Dr Hadwen, who had been recruited into the anti-vivisection movement by Frances Power Cobbe, the issues of anti-vivisection and anti-vaccination became inextricably linked. Although he was much liked by the citizens of Gloucester he was disliked by his medical colleagues who found his views 'far too radical for their comfort'.[43]

As a qualified and practising doctor, pro-vivisectionists could not denounce Dr Hadwen as well-meaning but uneducated. On the contrary, he had been awarded a scholarship at medical college for being the most distinguished student in his year. Hadwen was a great public speaker and was always prepared to enter into debate. His oratory skill and medical knowledge meant that he was able to run rings around his opponents and he was hated for it. George Bernard Shaw complimented him on his oratory skill, and called him the 'unanswerable Hadwen'. He was barred from membership of the British Medical Association and the manslaughter charge was seen as an attempt to prevent him practising medicine altogether.

Events in Gloucester: 1923

Although Hadwen's 'unorthodox and uncompromising views' were well known to fellow practitioners, there had been no particular friction since the epidemic of 1896. He was Chairman of the Gloucester Medical and Panel Committee which was evidence of the esteem in which he was held locally. However in 1923 Gloucester suffered another outbreak of smallpox and out of diplomacy Hadwen did not seek re-election of the Chair although he saw no need to relinquish membership of the Committee.

After the epidemic had become a thing of the past,

Dr Ellis, who argued that Nellie had died of diptheria

friendly relations were re-established with all but a handful of doctors who resented his continuing membership of the Committee and wanted to see him resign altogether. The leader of this faction was Dr Ellis and the animosity between the two doctors was well known. It was Ellis who was to play a key role in the charge brought against Hadwen following the death of Nellie Burnham.

The case of Nellie Burnham

On 1 August 1924, Dr Hadwen visited his patient Nellie Burnham and diagnosed ulcerative tonsillitis. Nellie was one of four children, two of whom had already been treated by Hadwen for the same illness. He visited Nellie again on 4 August and by 6 August he was 'delighted with her progress'. Mrs Burnham, the child's mother, told Hadwen that her daughter was much better and was sitting up in bed 'bright and smiling'. He was due to visit Nellie again on 8 August but had several urgent cases to deal with. As Nellie's case was not

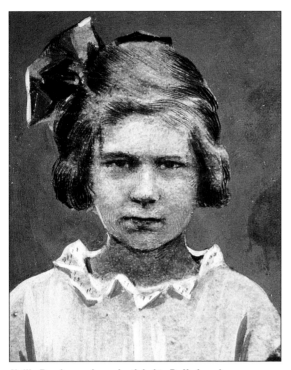

Nellie Burnham, whose death led to Dr Hadwen's manslaughter charge

Nellie's family: Mr Fudge (uncle), Mrs Burnham (mother) and Leonard (brother)

urgent, he postponed his visit to the following day.

The next day, as he was leaving the surgery to visit Nellie, her elder brother Leonard ran in begging Dr Hadwen to come at once as she had become much worse. Hadwen said in court that he was 'thunderstruck at the change in her' and saw that she had developed pneumonia. He did not prescribe any medicine. Hadwen believed that she would pull through with 'assiduous attention' and he spent the rest of the day in routine duties.

When he returned home that evening, he received a telephone call from a man he took to be the child's father. The caller said that he was dissatisfied with Nellie's treatment and was going to call in another doctor. Hadwen privately did not agree with this course of action, but he did not object. The telephone call turned out to be from Mrs Burnham's brother-in-law, Mr Fudge, who was visiting the family from Birmingham. The doctor he called in was Dr Ellis (Mr Fudge had been a patient of Dr Ellis when he lived in Gloucester).

The Coroner's inquest

The following week Dr Hadwen received a message from the Coroner asking if he would like to attend the inquest on Nellie Burnham as a post-mortem had been held and very serious charges were preferred against him. It was indicated that he should be accompanied by a solicitor. Up till then, Hadwen had not even been aware that Nellie had died as the case had been taken out of his hands.

At the inquest he heard that Dr Ellis had diagnosed diphtheria and alleged that the child's throat had been full of diphtheric membrane. Hadwen was staggered as he had examined her throat the same morning and had found no membrane at all. Ellis had refused to sign a death certificate on the grounds that he had not attend-

Crowds waiting expectantly outside the court for the verdict

ed the patient in her last illness and this necessitated a Coroner's inquest.

The post-mortem was carried out by Dr Washbourn, a personal friend of Dr Ellis. He certified that death was due to 'diphtheria and pneumonia' although he found no membrane in the throat which he admitted at the inquest that he 'would have expected' to see. Dr Washbourn admitted in court that he knew Dr Hadwen was charged with an error in diagnosis. (As a personal friend of Dr Ellis, however, the Union felt that Washbourn could not take an objective position.) Washbourn also said that the pneumonia was that which he would expect to find following exposure to a sudden chill. Hadwen had suspected that Nellie had had a sudden chill but her mother had denied this.

After the evidence had been heard against Dr Hadwen the inquiry was postponed for a month. Hadwen protested vigorously at this delay as it meant that although charges had been made against him he hadn't had the opportunity to defend himself. Yet in spite of the allegations remaining unanswered he claimed that not one patient left his practice.

New 'truly providential' evidence comes to light

The delay, however, turned out to be a 'blessing in disguise' for it brought to light a fact which Hadwen had always suspected, but for which there had been no evidence. He learnt how Nellie Burnham contracted the chill which brought on the pneumonia from which she died.

A man named Mr Tanner approached Hadwen after reading a report of Mrs Burnham's evidence at the inquest in the local paper. He said he felt it was only right to come forward as her report was, to his knowledge, untrue. Mr Tanner, a neighbour of the Burnham family, testified that Mrs Burnham had told him and his wife that Nellie had got out of bed and walked downstairs in her night-dress and bare feet, along a tiled passage into the kitchen, and then into the scullery where

Court scene from the trial of Dr Hadwen, October 1924

she had obtained cold water from the tap.

This evidence was 'truly providential' and was used in Hadwen's defence. Mrs Burnham was asked again if she could think of any circumstance which could have caused Nellie to contract a chill. She replied that she could not. When confronted with Mr Tanner's evidence

Court scene from the trial of Dr Hadwen, October 1924 (Dr Hadwen in the foreground)

she shouted 'He is a liar', but ultimately confessed that the conversation Tanner referred to had taken place.

In spite of the strength of Hadwen's case, nine men of the jury selected by the Coroner's Officer gave a verdict against him. The case was then brought before the magistrates' court on 2 October. A letter from Dr Ellis was published in the local press, which showed evidence of his animosity towards Dr Hadwen, but this only strengthened public opinion in Hadwen's favour. His opponents were fearful that they might not be able to get an impartial hearing in Gloucester because of his popularity and requested that the hearing be moved to London. However, Mr Justice Avory remarked that if a man had made a reputation for himself and 'won local esteem' then he was entitled to such benefit as may 'accrue therefrom'. The appeal to move the case was turned down as 'improper'.

Five thousand people wait for the verdict

The trial took place in Gloucester on 27, 28 and 29 October 1924. After the evidence was heard it took the jury just 20 minutes to reach a majority verdict acquitting Dr Hadwen. Outside, in the pouring rain, some 5,000 people were waiting for the verdict and they 'went mad' when it was known. The day of the verdict coincided with polling day in Gloucester but the people 'cared for little else than the restoration to complete freedom of their beloved doctor'.[44] Hadwen was besieged by well-wishers when he left the court and although he was weary after the trial he went on to Albion Hall where he addressed the crowd. The people of Gloucester greeted his acquittal with enormous relief and within half an hour of the verdict being known Dr Hadwen had received 250 telegrams of support.

The crowds waiting oustide the court

The case was widely reported in the press and the British Union published a verbatim report of the proceedings. The cost of the defence had been great but a special fund was established which soon raised more than enough money to cover the legal expenses of the trial.

Dr Hadwen's supporters felt that the whole affair had been nothing more than an deliberate attempt by certain members of the medical lobby to discredit his professional reputation and 'possibly even to remove this anti-vivisectionist from their midst'.[45] The powerful force of pro-vivisectionists had been seen before in the passing of the Cruelty to Animals Act 1876. Now perhaps they saw a golden opportunity not only to discredit Hadwen but to weaken the anti-vivisection movement as a whole. Hadwen's supporters argued that Nellie's death would have passed unnoticed if it had not been for the fact that Dr Hadwen was an anti-vivisectionist.

The crowds cheering Dr Hadwen after his acquittal

CHAPTER 8

The 1930s

A decade of change: new campaigning methods for a new era

The 1920s had been a highly contentious era for anti-vivisectionists and the annual public meetings held by the British Union were disrupted by medical students in scenes reminiscent of the brown dog era. George Bernard Shaw never spoke again at a meeting on behalf of the society following the strain of incessant interruptions when he addressed a public meeting in June 1927. The annual meeting in 1929 was broken up by the 'scandalous behaviour' of medical students. People were knocked down and trampled on, chairs and other furniture were damaged, and the speakers could not be heard above the shouting. In contrast, the years of the 1930s were much calmer and can be seen as a 'decade of change'.

Campaigning continues with 'unabating vigour'

Despite a less contentious atmosphere the Union's campaigns carried on with 'unabating vigour'. The shop campaigns continued and in an attempt to modernise them the old vivisection instruments and stuffed animal models, which had always been a key feature of any window display, were withdrawn. These were replaced with new models considered to be more representative of current vivisection practices. Campaign shops were opened in some of London's principal thoroughfares including Whitehall, Leicester Square, Regent Street and Oxford Street and a permanent shop was established in Scarborough. A kiosk was also used for several years in a shopping arcade just off The Strand. The van campaigns continued and three new vans were put on the road in 1938, two of which were fitted with loudspeakers.

There was an increase in the level of press advertising and an electronic news sign could be seen for six months at Charing Cross Station. *The Abolitionist* reached a circulation of over 16,000 a month and could be bought at over 20 different locations in the city. Posters were an essential tool to catch public attention

and the Union adopted a method whereby one poster message would be displayed simultaneously across the country. This obviously required the close co-operation of all branches. Posters could be seen in tube stations, on the sides of campaign vans, on sandwich boards and at post offices. A one-year contract was set up with WH Smith for a poster of *The Abolitionist* to be displayed on some of its bookstalls.

The Union also tested out the idea of focused campaigning activities in just one county for one month at a time, to saturate the chosen area with anti-vivisection propaganda. This experimental campaigning technique

Poster for the month of July 1938

BUAV campaign van in London, 1934

took place in July 1938 in Sussex. The campaign was hampered by stormy weather, and there was no clear feedback that this was an especially successful campaigning technique. It was nevertheless agreed that a second county should be tried out. A campaign was planned for Yorkshire but did not take place because of the outbreak of the Second World War in 1939.

Parliamentary work: the key to abolition

Parliamentary intervention was still regarded as the key to the eventual abolition of vivisection. Through the 1930s the Union presented no less than five petitions calling for experiments on living animals to be prohibited by law. The petitions reflected a gradual increase in the supporters of the cause: the last petition in 1939 carried more than twice as many signatures as the first in 1930. Mr Tom Groves was the new Parliamentary Representative of the Union and was responsible for presenting the petitions to the House of Commons. His political campaigning on behalf of the Union also included depositing his copy of *The Abolitionist* in the House of Commons library.

A general election was held in 1935 and although it did not lead to an increase of anti-vivisectionists in the House of Commons it did offer a 'glorious opportunity for publicity'. The theory behind the Union's parliamentary work was first to educate the public, and thereby convert the electorate to the anti-vivisection view. The electorate would then return candidates to the House who would vote in favour of an abolition Bill. Committed anti-vivisectionists were prepared to vote for a supportive candidate irrespective of party allegiance.

But by the late 1930s the matter of national defence had so absorbed the attention of the government that the time was regarded as inopportune for introducing such a Bill. The already 'archaic' 1876 Act was to remain on the statute books for another half century.

MacGregor v the British Union for the Abolition of Vivisection

In 1931 Mr Alasdair Alpin MacGregor, a member of the Union, made an 'unfounded attack' against the officials of the Union. As an anti-vivisectionist, MacGregor had returned his graduation diploma to the University of Edinburgh refusing to accept it from a place licensed for vivisection. But he believed that animal societies needed 'cleaning up'. He accused members of the Executive Committee - Dr Hadwen, Miss Kidd and Mr de Vere

Mr Tom Groves MP (BUAV Parliamentary Representative) and Mr Howard Cummins (BUAV organiser) with a petition calling for the abolition of vivisection, 8 February 1934

Summers - of scheming to disarm him as an anti-vivisection candidate for the RSPCA.

MacGregor felt that Dr Hadwen had thwarted his attempt to become a member of the Council of the RSPCA because Hadwen thought that the RSPCA should not undertake anti-vivisection campaigns as its primary focus was to deal with illegal cruelty to animals. Anti-vivisection societies, on the other hand, dealt with legal cruelty and he felt it best that this type of work should be left to the specialist societies.

Mr MacGregor had produced a leaflet which was regarded as 'grossly fictitious statements and insinuations' about the management of the Union. He distributed copies at the annual meeting in 1932 and at some of the branch meetings. Seen as a 'disturber of the peace' he was expelled as a Union member.

MacGregor subsequently tried to claim damages against the Union alleging that he had been illegally expelled and that libels had been published against him in *The Abolitionist*. The British Union defence argued that the expulsion had been lawful and that the alleged libels were actually answers to criticisms made by Mac-Gregor, and that they were 'fair comment' and of pub-

lic interest. The British Union believed that attacks against its officials should not be accepted without enquiry and that slanders should be met by a published statement so that evidence could be compared.

The case was heard in the High Court of Justice for three days beginning on 19 February 1935. On the third day the case came to an abrupt end when MacGregor, on the advice of his counsel, withdrew his charges against the Union and apologised for making such charges. He also said that his membership of the Union had been properly determined and he no longer wished to seek a declaration that he was still a member. The judge accepted that in view of the opinions MacGregor had expressed in court it would not have been in the best interests of the society to have him reinstated as a member, and the case was dismissed. The Union felt that the whole case had been nothing more than a distraction of time and money, using resources which could otherwise have been diverted into the campaigning funds of the society.

Death of Dr Hadwen: tireless campaigner for over 30 years

Walter Hadwen died at home on the evening of 27 December 1932, aged 78. He was buried a few days later in Gloucester Cemetery when the popularity and respect that he had achieved throughout his life was evident for all to see. Thousands of people lined the streets of Gloucester to pay their last respects, but those who waited outside his surgery for a final good-bye were to be disappointed as the funeral procession was re-routed by the police to avoid congestion in the city. All but one of the London newspapers carried an obituary notice and the provincial newspapers were flooded with them.

Dr Hadwen, who had succeeded Frances Power Cobbe as the leader of the British Union, had worked tirelessly for the anti-vivisection cause for over 30 years. All this work was unpaid, and in addition to his work as a doctor and a magistrate. Hadwen was succeeded as President of the British Union by Leonora, Countess of Tankerville.

The last service which Dr Hadwen performed on behalf of the Union was to lead a deputation to the Director of Talks at the British Broadcasting Corporation (BBC). He asked for the anti-vivisection case to be heard in a radio debate: the Union felt the issue of vivi-

Presentation of BUAV's petition to Parliament to abolish vivisection, 1 March 1939

section was being unfairly vetoed by the BBC's refusal to discuss a matter which it deemed too controversial.

Radio: a potential medium for airing anti-vivisection arguments

Radio was a popular form of entertainment in the 1930s and was listened to in most homes. However, although discussions about medical developments and practices were frequently aired, and so-called 'experts' were freely permitted to broadcast their opinions, the BBC considered that the issue of vivisection was too controversial to be discussed. This policy worried the British Union as it meant that 'grotesque misrepresentations' went unchallenged.

The BBC declined the suggestion of holding a debate on vivisection as it did with other issues as 'it is a subject the discussion of which raises such bitter feeling that we feel it wisest not to deal with it in our programmes'.[46] At the annual council meeting of 1932 a resolution was passed that the Union should write to the BBC asking it to receive a deputation about its attitude in denying an opportunity for airing the anti-vivisection point of view.

This deputation, headed by Dr Hadwen, met with Mr Siepmann, the Director of Talks, at BBC headquarters on 29 September 1932. Hadwen claimed that 'it was only a matter of justice and fair play' that the anti-vivisection case should be heard too, as well as the other side of the debate. He argued that anti-vivisection could no longer be regarded as the fad of a few and it was distressing to those who held strong views that they were debarred from answering inaccurate statements. The deputation gave an assurance that its case would be presented in a 'temperate' style, that it would not mention the names of any living people and that it would make every effort to avoid offence.

The Director of Talks replied that nobody had a 'right' to express their opinions through the BBC but he did accept that significant issues had been raised and the deputation felt assured that the issue would receive consideration. Mr Siepmann had, however, stipulated that no air time would be given to a discussion of vivisection from either a moral or a scientific standpoint. Members of the Executive Committee replied that if they were to be debarred from broadcasting their views then the BBC should, in common fairness, give an assurance that pro-vivisectionists would not be allowed to advocate vivisection or the resulting practice of vaccination. Although no such assurance was given, the British Union was pleased to note that a series of health talks shortly afterwards made no mention of vivisection or vaccination. This practice turned out to be short-lived and was probably no more than a short-term effort to appease the Union.

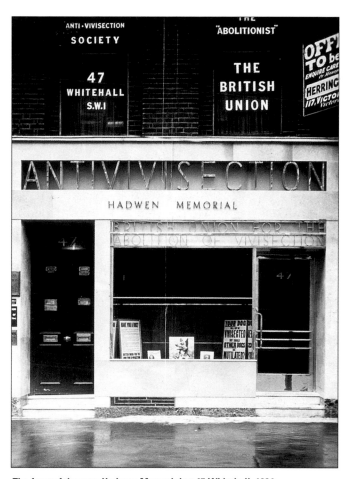

The front of the new Hadwen Memorial at 47 Whitehall, 1934

Not willing to give in easily the British Union again asked the BBC, in December 1932, to reconsider its decision and to allow a broadcast presenting the Union's case. The Union supported its claim by revealing that more people were actually opposed to vaccination than in favour of it. In 1930 more parents had made use of the conscientious clause to obtain exemption certificates, by making a declaration of conscientious objection against vaccination before a magistrate, than had actually had their babies vaccinated.

At this point the Director General wrote to the British Union to say that the BBC would shortly be putting forward a proposal for consideration. In January 1933 a definite promise was made for a debate to be

held on vivisection and the British Union expressed appreciation at what had been a major concession by the BBC.

The debate took place on 25 March 1933 and was part of a series called *Should They Be Scrapped?* Reverend Walter Long of the British Union's Executive Committee spoke in favour of the abolition of vivisection while the opposing view was put by Professor AV Hill of University College, London. The Radio Times reported that the protagonists would be in separate studios, although whether this was for technical reasons or because of fears that they might 'set about each other' was not explained. The debate was anticipated to be one of the most controversial yet broadcast.

The debate however passed without incident and a verbatim report was printed in the May edition of *The Abolitionist*.

The debate turned out to be a one-off broadcast. After that, vivisection returned to the 'black-list' at Broadcasting House and it could not be referred to, either directly or indirectly, without first gaining special permission. In response to the British Union's requests for further debates, the Director of Talks replied that there were no plans to hold any debates on vivisection but if the BBC was to change its mind it would contact the organisation beforehand. The British Union realised that this was unlikely to happen unless the public demanded it, and supporters were asked to write to the BBC expressing their opinion on the matter.

Throughout the rest of the decade the BBC would hold no further debate on vivisection and the British Union began to look for a radio station overseas to publicise its cause. The Union eventually had to concede that radio as a means of promoting the cause 'is completely debarred to us' after refusals came from both Radio Luxembourg and Radio Normandy.

The Hadwen Memorial: a permanent centre of propaganda

In 1931 the address of the British Union headquarters became 47 Whitehall, London. Although this suggests a change of premises, it was actually due to the street being renamed. Charing Cross had often been confused with Charing Cross Road and the authorities decided to give it a new name. The Union was initially opposed to this suggestion because of the costs involved in reprinting all its leaflets with a new address. It later welcomed the change when it realised how many potential visitors had been unable to find the office because of the confusion in street names.

The Union had been eager to pay tribute to its dedicated President with some sort of memorial. Several suggestions were made including the erection of a bronze statue of Dr Hadwen in the City of Gloucester. Eventually it was decided that a permanent shop at 47 Whitehall, with a hall for meetings at the back, would make a fitting memorial. This established a permanent centre of propaganda for the anti-vivisection movement.

The Hadwen Memorial was opened on 10 December 1934 by Dr Hadwen's eldest daughter, Mrs Una Rodenhurst, and was staffed by one of the Union's organisers Mr Maurice Toms. The proximity of the memorial to government offices and the Houses of Parliament meant that it brought the question of vivisection to the constant attention of politicians and officials in a very striking way and, as Mrs Rodenhurst said: 'What could be more fitting than to emphasise my father's long association with Whitehall?'[47] The Hadwen Memorial became a focus for anti-vivisection visitors from all over the world. Its window display was changed frequently and became one of the best known in London.

CHAPTER 9

The second world war years

The Union maintains momentum, despite wartime restrictions

The outbreak of war in late 1939 once again restricted campaigning activities, and in the 1940s it became necessary to adjust 'daily habits' to wartime conditions. The Union refrained from commenting on the war itself except where it was relevant to the anti-vivisection movement. Vaccination was again a major issue throughout these years but other campaigns were also undertaken. The Union did not cease its activities throughout the war despite the restriction of essential resources such as paper and petrol, and the need to abandon its London headquarters temporarily after a bomb raid.

The Union hoped that the restrictions placed on its work would also affect the practice of vivisection, and that the practice would be curtailed (although, realistically, it knew that this was 'hardly probable'). Vivisection continued to increase and by 1943 over one million experiments were being performed each year.

Evacuation of London headquarters

Work had carried on from Union headquarters at the Hadwen Memorial, 47 Whitehall, for more than a year after the outbreak of war. This, however, was becoming increasingly difficult and dangerous because of air raids, and the government advised that those who could do so should leave London and conduct their business from elsewhere.

In October 1940 the Hadwen Memorial was badly damaged during an enemy attack and the Executive Committee decided that it would be in the Union's best interests to transfer its headquarters to a place where work would be safer and less likely to be interrupted. One member of staff who had been in the office at the time of the attack made a lucky escape. Even in these trying circumstances the British Union lost no opportunity to promote its cause: when the broken windows of 47 Whitehall had to be boarded up they were covered with large propaganda posters and notices to inform the public of the new location.

Offices were found in Hereford and the temporary headquarters of the Union registered at Imperial Chambers, 138 Widemarsh Street. Most Executive Committee meetings were held there, although the AGM continued to be held in London.

The ground floor of 47 Whitehall had not been as badly damaged as the first floor. The necessary repairs were carried out and the furniture replaced. The ground floor was re-opened just one year later, in October 1941, and Executive Committee meetings once again returned to the Hadwen Memorial. The remaining first floor offices were not re-occupied until after the end of the war in August 1945 when the headquarters returned to its home at 47 Whitehall. In 1949 the British Union purchased the premises at 47-51 Whitehall where it had rented office space for its headquarters since first moving to London in 1905.

Other wartime restrictions

Paper was a valuable commodity during the war and *The Abolitionist* had to be reduced from a monthly to a bi-monthly publication. The circulation of the journal fell from 16,000 to 8,000 as subscriptions from overseas were lost; the general upheaval also meant that many subscribers could not be traced. One other commodity which had been essential to the work of the Union, and which was now diminished, was that of volunteers.

The van campaigns had to be reduced because of petrol rationing and, once again, it became difficult to find suitable locations for the shop campaigns, although they didn't stop altogether. One of the Union's campaign vans was requisitioned by the Ministry of Transport and, although the other vans were kept by the Union, the withdrawal of petrol supplies meant that the van campaigns stopped in June 1943.

The headquarters of the Manchester branch along with all its records were completely destroyed during an air raid. Compensation was received from the government and a new building was purchased at 65

Cartoon from *The Abolitionist*, 1945

Upper Chorlton Road. This was used both as the branch headquarters and as an anti-vivisection centre along the same lines as the Hadwen Memorial in London. The property was renamed Hadwen House making it the second of the Union's premises with that name (the first had been established by the Liverpool branch in 1929).

The ban on Private Members' Bills in the House of Commons meant that the Union was not able to put forward any of its proposed legislation and had to satisfy itself with other methods, such as petitions, to keep the issue alive in Parliament. The Home Secretary announced that the annual returns of experiments on living animals would not be published for the duration of the war. This was yet another hindrance as the statistics gave valuable information about the number and types of experiments being carried out, where and by whom.

The branches continued their work under extremely difficult conditions and were drastically short of voluntary helpers. The Union felt strongly that it was essential to keep branches functioning so that there would be a base in every district from which to commence post-war campaigns.

Union publicity drive about voluntary vaccination policy

During the First World War the Union had focused its campaigning activities almost exclusively on vaccination and the Union was quick to take this issue up again when the Second World War broke out. It sought assurance from the government, via parliamentary questions, that vaccination would not be compulsory for new recruits who joined up for the war.

Having received this assurance, the Union then tried to exert pressure on the government to advertise the fact. It argued that if soldiers did not know about their right to refuse, then they would be under the impression that vaccination was obligatory and would have no opportunity to make their own decision. The Union also took up the cases of soldiers who had been subjected to improper pressure and who had been penalised for refusing to be vaccinated.

The government, however, declined to promote the policy actively and so, once again, the Union decided to advertise it instead. Posters were produced quoting the Secretary of State for War declaring that vaccination was not compulsory. These posters were displayed extensively and men with sandwich boards were employed to parade with them outside the London labour exchanges on army recruitment days. Leaflets were also distributed to new recruits all over the country.

Wartime experiments: 'never practised more revoltingly'

The British Union's prediction that it seemed 'hardly probable' that the war would also curtail the experimental activities of scientists was proved right. In fact

vivisection was never practised more revoltingly than it was during the Second World War.[48]

Horses, which had served in the forces and were no longer fit for action, were retired to the laboratory. Here they would be used for manufacturing anti-toxin serum. After protests from the British Union the reply received from a question in the House of Commons was that 'for technical reasons' these army horses were the most suitable for this purpose and that the process involved no cruelty.

In Britain, warfare experiments were conducted at Porton Down in Wiltshire, first established as the War Department Experimental Ground during the First World War in 1916. Experiments conducted were even more secretive than usual as the results were regarded as matters of national security. Here, animals of all species were used in experiments to observe the

Horses were used in laboratories to produce anti-toxin. Painting by Fritz Gehrke

effects of poisonous gases and chemicals, and in wounding experiments where animals were shot to see the resulting blast injuries. Other animals were burnt, irradiated, infected with gangrene and exposed to other forms of traumatic shock.

In 1942 Porton scientists were responsible for supervising experiments to test anthrax bombs. This involved shipping about 30 sheep to Gruinard, a remote Scottish island, and exploding an anthrax bomb. All the sheep died within a week. The island was only decontaminated in 1986, over 40 years after exposure to this lethal gas.

The American Embassy was bombarded with letters of protest about government plans to use live animals in atomic bomb tests, due to take place on 1 July 1946 in the Pacific Ocean. Appeals to President Truman against putting animals on ships which were to be bombed went unheard. The Conference of Anti-Vivisection Societies, of which the British Union was a member, also passed a resolution protesting to the United Nations about the proposed experiments. It argued that such experiments could undermine public confidence in the United Nations as an instrument for the preservation of peace.

However, despite all appeals and protests, the experiments went ahead at the scheduled time. There were an estimated 3,519 animals on board the ships, including tethered goats, pigs and sheep.

CHAPTER 10

The 1940s

Working together for a common cause

The Second World War appeared to foster a greater notion of co-operation within the anti-vivisection movement. It was felt that it would be more advantageous for the anti-vivisection societies to work in harmony for the sake of the cause: there was a realisation that nothing could be gained from warfare among the societies. In the decade in which the Union celebrated its 50th birthday, the campaign against the BBC for freedom of speech was continued and an end to compulsory vaccination was achieved. The Union established a Youth Section but lost its charitable status.

Conference of Anti-Vivisection Societies: a vehicle for joint action

At the invitation of the British Union, representatives from six anti-vivisection societies met on 20 November 1942 at Caxton Hall, Westminster. The meeting was arranged

for the purpose of discussing and making plans for a joint intensive campaign, after the war, to claim the total abolition of vivisection as a necessary step toward securing for animals their rightful place in the new world order, which is generally believed will follow the peace.[49]

Members of the Conference met regularly and provided a vehicle for the societies to take joint action on a number of matters. Many of the issues addressed were those on which the British Union had already been campaigning. The British Union felt that

this linking up with other organisations has proved fruitful in many ways, and has been done without any loss of independence or modification in policy.[50]

On 23 February 1948 Mr Ronald Chamberlain, one of the Union's official parliamentary supporters, led a deputation from the Conference to put forward views

about the failures of the 1876 Act to the Home Secretary. The deputation went to ask for the appointment of a third Royal Commission to consider the practice of present-day vivisection and to oppose the recent request made to the Home Secretary by vivisectors to allow stray cats and dogs to be made available to them.

Mr Chuter Ede, the Home Secretary, stated that he had refused the request about use of stray cats and dogs. He promised to consider the request made by the deputation for the appointment of a Royal Commission and to send an official reply in due course. However, a reply dated 9 June 1948 stated that there was 'no sufficient case' to justify the appointment of a Royal Commission.

The Conference adopted the British Union's draft Bill for the prohibition of vivisection but even after the 1945 general election, when Clement Attlee was elected Prime Minister, there was still a ban on Private Members' Bills in the House of Commons. However the Conference had a final draft of a Bill which would be ready when the time came, with the added advantage of having the weight of all the anti-vivisection societies behind it.

Further campaigns for freedom of speech

The British Union had previously protested to the BBC about the inclusion of controversial theories in talks on medical subjects and the fact that no speaker was ever allowed to disprove them. The BBC explained that it was guided by authoritative advice from the Ministry of Health and that it would continue to abide by this advice.

The BBC's charter, which gave it a monopoly over radio broadcasting, was due to expire at the end of 1946. The British Union felt that if it was to be renewed it should be with the stipulation that both sides of controversial subjects should be broadcast. A poster on the freedom of speech was published. A letter was written to MPs about the renewal of the BBC charter pointing

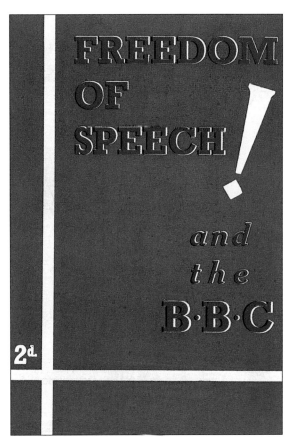

BUAV protested against the BBC's refusal to debate vivisection

Digger, who was saved from vivisection by his owner's determination

out the bias constantly shown towards vivisection in radio programmes dealing with health matters. The British Union was concerned that the BBC had a 'one-sided method of dealing with the problems of disease'. However it appears that the campaign was not successful as the debate continued after the end of 1946.

A further deputation from the British Union was received at Broadcasting House in June 1948 by the Director of the Spoken Word, Mr Barnes. No programme dealing specifically with vivisection was to be arranged although he did state that he was not opposed to the topic being introduced into other programmes. A debate did eventually take place on 3 March 1949, broadcast from the Midland Regional Station. The British Union expressed its hopes that this would not be an isolated concession, as had happened previously, and hoped that it was in fact an indication of a more liberal attitude on the part of the BBC. However, a further debate arranged for June 1949, on which the British Union had been consulted to help write the script, was cancelled a week before it was due to be broadcast. All protests were in vain.

Digger's tale

In May 1945, Mr Bailey of Bradford lost his dog Digger, a three-year-old schipperke, and went to see Mrs Clayton Smith, Secretary of the Bradford branch for help. She advised him to call on a Mr Dracup who had a reputation for dealing in stolen pets but, despite being given a full description of Digger, Mr Dracup claimed

What Boys and Girls can do.

ANIMALS need your **help**. They are often very badly treated. For instance, there is a cruel practice called "Vivisection," which means experiments upon living animals. In some of these experiments animals are starved, or have poisons put into them, or are made very ill through operations they do not need.

You all know what it means to be hurt, and that it is hard to bear the pain, even when someone hurts you just for fun. You probably cry out, and say "It hurts!" But when animals, or birds, or insects, are made to suffer pain, they cannot speak and tell you how much it hurts.

If you think over all the things animals do for us—the work dogs and horses do, the pleasure and love our dogs and cats give us — you will never be able to

FLORENCE NIGHTINGALE'S
The dog had an injured leg, and
going to kill it, but Florence became
saved its life.

In the 1940s a Youth Section was established and materials aimed specifically at children were published

To Boys and Girls

A LEAFLET FOR CHILDREN

"VIVISECTION"

WHAT IT MEANS

that he couldn't help Mr Bailey. Bailey was then advised to go to Bradford railway station the following Thursday as that was the day that Dracup sent batches of dogs down to London to the laboratory that he worked for.

Mr Bailey claimed that he recognised the sound of Digger's bark coming from one of the crates marked for delivery to Burroughs Wellcome laboratory and demanded that the case was opened. Inside was Digger.

Following this, and another similar incident, Mrs Clayton Smith wrote a leaflet called *Bradford Citizens, Watch Your Dogs* which led to her being sued for libel. The case, lasting three days, was heard at Leeds Assizes in April 1947 and brought to light the huge trade in which the dealer was involved. Dracup admitted that he had been selling dogs to Wellcome for the previous 12 years and, as he was guaranteed a minimum of 17s 6d for each dog, it was a lucrative business for him.

The jury found that the leaflet contained defamatory matter that was not shown to be true. It ruled in favour of Dracup who was awarded £500 damages. The British Union appealed against the verdict but without success. The whole case cost over £2,000 but extensive publicity had been achieved as the case was widely reported in the press, awakening sympathy for the cause.

The Executive Committee agreed that Mrs Clayton Smith should be indemnified and that the Union would bear the legal costs. A special appeal fund was established so that the costs would not come out of general appeal funds. It was decided that in future all branch publications should be checked by headquarters to avoid such a situation happening again.

Youth Section: increasing interest from children

An increased interest in the anti-vivisection issue from

Miss Beatrice Kidd, BUAV President 1948 to 1958

children led to some of the branches setting up their own junior sections. Mrs Ada Barnett of the Executive Committee inaugurated the idea in 1944 recognising that 'we old ones cannot live forever'. She sent a recommendation to branches encouraging them to establish youth sections and to make every effort to bring young people into the society. A Junior Section news sheet was produced for the first time in April 1945 edited by Mrs Stella Lief. This soon progressed into a printed journal with a circulation of about 1,000 copies.

Membership of the Youth Section (as it was renamed) increased rapidly and by 1949 there were about 3,000 members. This influx of young supporters was seen as an 'encouraging sign' and a Youth Executive Committee was established. The Youth Section held its own meetings, quizzes and lectures and it also ran an annual summer holiday camp to enable young people to combine education with fun. The first camp, attended by 30 boys and girls, was held in the summer of 1949 at Biggin Hill in Kent.

The National Health Service - and an end to compulsory vaccination

The National Health Service Act of 1946 'records a triumph for our cause' as it repealed the previous Acts which had made the practice of vaccination compulsory since 1853. Parents were no longer required to make declarations of objection if they did not wish their children to be vaccinated. The anti-vaccinationists had been campaigning for this change for almost a century and the issue had become entrenched in the anti-vivisection movement under the presidency of Dr Hadwen. The Ministry of Health had at last 'bowed to the force of public opinion'.

The British Union had argued for many years that it was the development of systems of public health, and not advances in medical science, which was responsible for the decline in all the major infectious diseases. The establishment of the National Health Service in 1948 was a major step forward in the involvement of the state in the provision of health services.

Charitable status withdrawn from all anti-vivisection societies

In 1947 the British Union and all anti-vivisection societies suffered a severe blow when it was ruled that they were no longer to be regarded as charitable organisations. The legal status of anti-vivisection societies as charities had been established by a legal ruling back in 1895 and had been recognised ever since. However the Inland Revenue challenged this granting of charitable status and made a test case by demanding payment of income tax from NAVS for the year ending 5 April 1943.

In the NAVS case, Special Commissioners concluded that a large amount of present-day medical and scientific knowledge was due to experiments on living animals and that 'many valuable cures for and preventatives of disease' had been discovered by such means. The Commissioners decided that these arguments far outweighed the advancement of morals and education that would be brought about by the abolition of vivisection as had been argued in 1895. The advantage of the continuation of vivisection therefore outweighed its abolition; an anti-vivisection stance was deemed to be against public interest, and therefore not charitable.

Although NAVS took the ruling to the House of Lords, the highest level of appeal, the case was dismissed with costs when it was heard on 2 July 1947.

The obvious impact of this was the loss of tax benefits, a privilege granted to charities. This considerable loss of revenue would obviously need to be offset against an increase in donations and subscriptions. The British Union was also worried about a possible loss of prestige through the loss of its charitable status.

BUAV: half a century of campaigning against cruelty

In June 1948 the British Union for the Abolition of Vivisection celebrated its 50th birthday. Leonora, Countess of Tankerville had resigned at the end of 1947 due to ill-health and at the July AGM in 1948 Miss Beatrice Kidd was elected as President. In 1949, after 50 years of publishing *The Abolitionist*, the British Union renamed its journal *The Anti-Vivisectionist*. The rationale behind the change was that the old title referred only to the policy of the organisation, not its aims. The former title had been adopted at a time when the policy of anti-vivisection societies was the subject of 'acute controversy' but it did not explain what exactly the Union wanted to abolish. The new title was 'forceful' and 'unmistakable' and left no doubt about what the society represented.

The British Union decided to abandon reference to its shortened title as it had led to some confusion with other societies with similar names, such as the British Union of Fascists. Having been established since 1898, and being known worldwide, it felt that to give up the name altogether 'would seem very much akin to lowering our flag'. Instead the society began to refer to itself as BUAV - an abbreviation still used to this day.

CHAPTER 11

1950s to 1970s

Emergence of animal liberation and animal welfare work

The 'sordid trade' of supplying pets to laboratories

BUAV had long been aware of the 'sordid trade' by which pets were supplied to laboratories but during recent years it had increased to such an alarming extent that during the 1950s and 1960s this campaign was stepped up. The Union became committed to a policy of rescuing and rehoming dogs otherwise destined for laboratories.

The trade in pet dogs was not always illegal as dogs were often supplied unwittingly by owners to dealers. The major laboratories often employed such dealers to provide them with the dogs they required for their experiments. The dealers obtained the dogs by placing adverts in local newspapers offering to find good homes for unwanted pets, or by visiting markets such

Mr JH English, whose work was the inspiration behind the 'Dog Rescue Campaign'

as Club Row in east London where dogs were openly traded.

The campaign began when one of the Union's area organisers, Mr JH English, began visiting the weekly animal sales at Melton Mowbray in Leicestershire where he would bid for dogs against a certain dealer. The dealer, after some weeks, seemed to give up the competition as a bad job. At this time, if homes could not be found for the dogs quite quickly, they were put to sleep humanely as there was nowhere else that they could be homed.

Doncaster was also a hot centre for the trade in dogs and volunteer workers kept a continuous watch for activity. As the trade was not illegal, it was important to educate the public about what might happen if they sold their dog to a stranger. A shop was offered rent-free for BUAV to run a campaign, and the Doncaster branch of the Union staged a demonstration at Doncaster central station on 10 May 1950 where a consignment of dogs awaited despatch to London. BUAV later hired a stall at Doncaster market which was used for distributing propaganda against the trade in dogs, together with general enlightenment on vivisection issues.

One of the earliest cases of the liberation of laboratory animals took place in Doncaster. A baker's labourer named Herbert Crawford went to the kennels of a known laboratory dealer and released eight dogs which were waiting for despatch to London. Crawford was charged at Doncaster Crown Court on 19 February 1952 with stealing two of the dogs and their collars. He was conditionally discharged, put on probation for two years and ordered to pay 18 shillings costs. In court Crawford defended his action because, as an anti-vivisectionist, it was his duty to prevent the dogs from reaching the laboratory and being used for experimental purposes. Fortunately, none of the dogs he released were returned to the dealer.

BUAV campaign uses the slogan 'Beware Cat Thieves'

Unlike the trade in dogs, which took place in open markets, BUAV could not intervene so easily in the trade in cats, as these were literally stolen off the streets in the middle of the night. This illegal trade was particularly 'endemic' in, although not exclusive to, London. A significant number of prosecutions against offenders took place, but the demand for cats was so great that it was always met.

The Union made every effort to counteract this growing trade by increasing public awareness. Posters were displayed with slogans such as 'Beware Cat Thieves' and advertisements were placed in local newspapers. An educational film *Like Unto You* was produced in conjunction with the British Conference of Anti-Vivisection Societies. The Union put pressure on those newspapers which accepted offending advertisements from dealers offering to rehome unwanted pets. In 1955 the Union introduced a £20 reward for information leading to the conviction of a cat thief. By 1965 this had increased to £250, and also applied to dogs.

The Research Defence Society had claimed in its journal *Conquest* that 'there is absolutely no evidence that laboratories receive stolen cats or have ever knowingly done so'.[51] However, no sooner had these words been printed than a man in Bodmin, in Cornwall, was convicted of stealing cats and supplying them to the School of Pharmacy in Bloomsbury Square, London.

Campaign to rescue dogs

The 'Dog Rescue Campaign' was established when the Executive Committee agreed to adopt the scheme inaugurated by Mr English whereby dogs destined for laboratories would be bought by BUAV and rehomed. A

BUAV published warnings against cat thieves

dog rescue fund was set up to meet the costs of this campaign. After illness prevented Mr English from pursuing this work, Mrs Scargall became the 'heroine' of the campaign. She would spend every Saturday, whatever the weather, at Doncaster market intercepting people who wanted to sell dogs before they reached the stall of a laboratory dealer.

In the first year the 'Dog Rescue Campaign' 'deprived' laboratories of over 400 dogs. While the number was small in relation to those they were not able to save, BUAV was doing something practical to end the trade. The campaign 'thoroughly annoyed' the enemy and hit them where it hurt by depriving them of what they regarded as the 'tools of their trade'.

In its first five years the 'Dog Rescue Campaign' saved about 2,750 dogs from laboratories. Most were found good homes. In Doncaster two local dogs homes were able to help find homes for the dogs and eventually BUAV bought its own property at 101 Colby Drive in Thurmaston, Leicester. Piggeries were converted into dog kennels where dogs could be housed in comfort while waiting for a new permanent home.

On 1 November 1950, BUAV held a demonstration at King's Cross station in London. The demonstrators met at headquarters first and then proceeded by three separate routes to the station to wait for the arrival of a train from the north which was carrying dogs destined for laboratories. At a pre-arranged signal the demonstrators unfurled their posters of protest and, dividing into two groups, marched round the station. The police eventually escorted the demonstrators off the premises.

Demonstration at King's Cross station, 1 November 1950

The following year two further demonstrations took place at King's Cross station, again targeting trains known to be carrying dogs. A public meeting was held on 24 March 1953 at Caxton Hall, London, to protest against the traffic in dogs to laboratories and the King's Cross demonstration was re-enacted. Demonstrators at the end of each row of seats unfurled their posters and marched onto the 'platform' where they stood in line with posters held high. A 'policeman' called on them to leave the 'station'.

The campaign received much valuable press publicity in both regional and national newspapers. *The People* newspaper agreed to make a thorough investigation into the trade in dogs to laboratories. A reporter went first to Doncaster where he watched the dealer buy the dogs. He then followed them back to the kennels and eventually boarded the train to London which was carrying the consignment of dogs. He tried to follow the van which collected them from King's Cross station but lost it in the heavy London traffic. However,

another reporter, who was waiting outside the laboratory, observed the van drive in and saw the dogs unloaded.

The BUAV Hendon and Aldenham Kennels were built in north London where rescued dogs from the market towns in the north were sent in weekly consignments after being met off the train at King's Cross station by kennel staff. Here they would receive any necessary veterinary treatment and await a new home. In an attempt to raise funds, branches were encouraged to adopt a kennel for £10 a year; a plaque bearing their name would be fixed over the kennel door. In 1962 the Nottingham branch presented the 'Dog Rescue Campaign' with a new van which was to be its 'pride and joy' and was used to make the weekly journey to King's Cross station to meet new consignments of rescued dogs.

Although the scheme was predominantly for dogs, it would rescue other types of animal from time to time, such as goats and foxes. One baby goat rescued

BUAV kennel staff collecting a new consignment of dogs from King's Cross station (Mr Sidney Hicks second from left)

from Thirsk market in north Yorkshire was to become the adopted pet of the Brixton branch in London and had a mascot coat specially made to fit. In 1965 the scheme was renamed Animal Rescue to reflect its willingness to help any animal in distress. The Animal Rescue Officer appointed was Sidney Hicks.

The Derek Roy Home-Finding Scheme for Retired Racing Greyhounds

The Daily Mirror was also supportive of BUAV campaigns. In October 1957 the newspaper, in conjunction with BUAV, Mr Derek Roy (a well-known comedian) and Mr Frank Sanderson launched a new home-finding scheme for retired racing greyhounds. An estimated 2,000 greyhounds were retired each year from racing tracks throughout the country: these were either destroyed or sold to vivisection laboratories.

BUAV wrote to all 72 licensed stadiums in the country asking for their co-operation in the scheme. It asked the stadiums to make use of the address file held by BUAV for prospective owners of retired dogs. Twenty-three agreed to co-operate with the scheme initially. Homes were found for over 100 dogs in the first three months. Before they were allowed a dog, prospective applicants had to complete a questionnaire and give assurances, that they were able to feed and exercise a dog, and that they were also willing to give it affection.

In 1966 a Greyhound Gala Night was held at the Hackney and Hendon Stadium in London on behalf of the Derek Roy Home-Finding Scheme for Retired

Racing Greyhounds. The aim was to combine racing with the opportunity to promote awareness of the Union's home-finding scheme and to raise funds.

The event was such a success that the General Manager promised to make it an annual event. The gala night was held again in 1967 when actor Leslie Phillips awarded the race prizes, and in 1968 when tickets for the prize draw were sold by a line-up of top fashion models including Celia Hammond and Joanna Lumley.

Leslie Phillips awarding the prizes at the Greyhound Gala Night, 1967

Top fashion models volunteer at the Greyhound Gala Night, 7 June 1968

Celebrities take the message to thousands

The Animal Stars Council was a group of stage, radio and television celebrities, headed by Derek Roy, who gave their support to BUAV's campaign. One of its most active members was top model, Celia Hammond. BUAV had a carnival float which toured the country during the summer months taking the anti-vivisection message to thousands of people. The combination of celebrities and mascot dogs was a great attraction and it often won a prize as one of the best floats in the carnival parade. Other members of the Council assisted by making pleas for homes for unwanted animals. These included well-known names such as Vera Lynn, Cliff Richard, Max Bygraves and Jayne Mansfield.

Branches were encouraged to adopt a rescued dog as a branch mascot, and dogs wearing BUAV coats were an excellent source of publicity at local events. The Hastings branch adopted Bobby, the dog seen in BUAV's promotional film *Anti-Vivisection by the Sea*, and headquarters adopted both a 'King and Queen' mascot. Derek Roy's old English sheepdog, Nero, became the King mascot of the campaign, and the Queen mascot was a rescued old English sheepdog called Misty.

In 1959 the 'Dog Rescue Campaign' was patroned

Celebrity supporter Joanna Lumley helps raise funds by selling raffle tickets at the Greyhound Gala Night, 7 June 1968

BUAV carnival float promoting the 'Dog Rescue Campaign' at Watford, 1961

BUAV carnival float at Southend, July 1966, with Tania Mallet (left), Misty and Celia Hammond (right)

Prince Rainier of Monaco receiving the presentation book depicting the work of the 'Dog Rescue Campaign' from Derek Roy, 1961

by His Serene Highness Prince Rainier of Monaco who had denounced vivisection as a 'semi-sadistic practice'. In 1961 Derek Roy flew to Monaco to meet Prince Rainier to thank him for his support and to present him with a specially prepared pictorial volume documenting the work of the campaign throughout 1960.

Humane solutions for stray cats and dogs

Claims from vivisectors that stray cats and dogs should be handed over to laboratories were not uncommon, but in Britain this was prohibited by law. BUAV had always opposed any such proposal but remained ever cautious since a similar campaign in the United States had already led to impounded dogs being supplied automatically to laboratories in some states.

BUAV argued that if such a law was passed in Britain, making it compulsory for stray animals to be handed over by animal shelters, these organisations would be placed in an 'impossible situation'. Funding from animal lovers would cease when they learnt of the

Sidney Hicks and BUAV campaign mascot Misty promoting the work of BUAV, 1950s

situation; the shelters would be forced to close down; and the vivisectors would have defeated their own ends. In response to public concern on this issue Battersea Dogs Home had long implemented a policy of refusing to supply dogs to laboratories.

Stray dogs were the responsibility of the police. Some police authorities would allow people wanting a pet to have one of their unclaimed dogs. One dealer began to take advantage of this situation and got a plentiful supply of free dogs which he then sold to laboratories. BUAV drew this matter to the attention of the Chief Constable who gave an assurance that no more dogs would be handed over to the man in question, or indeed to anyone else suspected of the same practice.

A parliamentary question made a case for legislation making it compulsory for laboratories purchasing live animals to maintain adequate records about their purchasing transactions. However, the Home Secretary, Mr Butler, replied that from the available evidence he could not see that the practice of stealing animals for sale to laboratories was widespread and was not satisfied that such legislation was necessary.

BUAV also wrote to the Home Secretary suggesting that pet shops should only be licensed if they undertook a commitment that no animals from the shop would be sold for experimental purposes. A badge was designed for pet shops to display in their window, which was only awarded after the shop had undertaken not to sell any pets for vivisection purposes.

In 1964 BUAV launched its own scheme to combat the serious problem of stray cats and dogs which some people felt should be sent to the vivisection laboratory.

NO ANIMALS ARE SOLD FOR VIVISECTION FROM THESE PREMISES

ISSUED   BY

B.U.A.V.

47. WHITEHALL S.W.I.

BUAV designed a sticker for those pet shops which pledged not to supply pets for vivisection

It advocated the practice of sterilisation of stray dogs as a positive step to reducing the number of unwanted dogs born each year. The ABC Fund was launched to raise money for owners who couldn't afford to pay for the operations themselves. BUAV was the first animal welfare society to advocate such a policy. In many ways, BUAV was not entirely comfortable with the policy. However, it saw the attempt to reduce the number of strays as a better solution than sending all stray animals to laboratories to await an even worse fate.

Over 25,000 animals rescued and rehomed

Eventually BUAV's work in rehoming animals, rehabili-

tating and rehoming retired greyhounds, and the promotion of a spaying and neutering scheme were all combined into the work of a single charity - the Animal Welfare Trust. The Trust was granted charitable status in 1971 and has operated as an independent organisation ever since. By 1975 it was estimated that since the inauguration of animal rescue work in the 1950s over 25,000 animals had been rescued and rehomed.

The work of rehoming retired greyhounds later became the responsibility of the professional body of the sport, the National Greyhound Racing Club. NGRC established its own Retired Greyhound Trust, work which is still carried out today by voluntary helpers.

CHAPTER 12

The 1950s

Coalitions and co-operation in campaigns against cruelty

Throughout the 1950s co-operation between the various societies continued and BUAV even considered a proposed merger with NAVS. The parliamentary climate was still not ripe for the introduction of an abolition Bill and the level of advertising had to be curtailed because of costs. However the press was becoming increasingly interested in the anti-vivisection issue and the publicity generated in this way helped to offset the decrease in advertising. Demonstrations, which had previously been held in town centres, became focused on the laboratory itself.

Coalitions and co-operation

There continued to be a level of greater understanding and closer co-operation between the various societies working on behalf of animals and the Conference of Anti-Vivisection Societies continued to maintain a 'spirit of friendliness, harmony and co-operation'. New co-operative bodies were also set up and, at one point, BUAV was participating in the work of five different joint bodies. Some of these were anti-vivisection coalitions and some were animal welfare coalitions; some were British and some were international.

A World Congress for the Protection of Animals was held in The Hague, Holland, in 1950. BUAV was represented by Mr Peter Turner, one of the Union's organisers, whose address consisted largely of a plea for anti-vivisection to be regarded as an integral part of animal welfare. The legal abolition of vivisection in all countries was adopted as a policy of the Congress. BUAV was therefore able to argue that its involvement helped to gain wider acceptance for the abolitionist principle. The official policy of BUAV was to co-operate with other animal welfare organisations as far as possible, while at the same time holding steadfastly to the principle of the total abolition of vivisection.

A World Congress of Animal Welfare Societies, organised by the British Federation of Animal Welfare Societies, was held in London between 17 and 19 May

1954. The Congress discussed all aspects of animal welfare and a special session was given over to the issue of vivisection. BUAV did eventually resign from the British Federation of Animal Welfare Societies as it felt the Federation 'seemed to serve no purpose that could not be served at least as well' by another of the coalitions to which the Union belonged, the Conference of Animal Welfare Societies.

At the AGM in 1958 a resolution was passed requesting the Executive Committee to explore the possibility of a fusion with NAVS. BUAV approached NAVS and it was agreed to hold a joint conference with four committee members from each society. The first meeting was held on 30 January 1959 at which two main points were considered: firstly, whether fusion between the societies was possible; and secondly, if it was possible, then how could this best be achieved.

The whole matter proved to be a great deal more complicated than had been anticipated. The financial aspect of the proposal in particular proved to be a 'substantial obstacle'. Eventually, at a further joint conference on 8 August 1959, it was decided to recommend that the idea of fusion should be dropped. Instead it was agreed that the two societies should find a way of working together more closely through a Joint Consultative Council. These recommendations were adopted by the committees of both societies and the first meeting of the Joint Consultative Council took place on 20 November 1959.

Parliamentary climate:
the 'hardest nut' to crack

Even in the 1950s it wasn't easy to influence the House of Commons. BUAV continued to do everything it could to influence the House legitimately and on 1 November 1950 Mr Peter Freeman MP handed in yet another BUAV petition to the House. BUAV continued its educational campaign among the electorate realising that to capture Parliament 'we must first capture the peo-

Demonstration in Salisbury market place, 1950s

ple; the ordinary men and women of our land'. Parliament was seen as the final stage of the battle, and time and money should not be wasted when the 'enemy has superior forces'.

The 1950 general election reduced BUAV's 26 official parliamentary supporters in the House to just 11. Its priority after the election was to raise this number so that it could introduce the Bill as soon as the time became opportune. It regarded the current House as likely to prove to be the 'hardest nut' it had yet to crack. It saw the key to the laboratories as being in the hands of the House of Commons, and the Commons as being in the hands of the voters. BUAV felt that it mattered little who the current Home Secretary was.

During the war the Home Office had stopped publishing annual returns on the number of animals used in experiments. Publication was resumed in 1949. However after the war the statistics were produced in a different format and did not include a list of the registered establishments or licensees; these had to be obtained separately from the Home Office. Now, the Home Secretary decided to stop publishing these 'vitally important sources of reference'. Loss of this information was seen as a serious handicap.

BUAV wrote to the Home Office suggesting that if the lists were not published each year, then the Home Office could instead produce a supplementary list showing any additions or deletions for that year. This proposal was rejected on the grounds that insufficient numbers of people were actually interested in the information. The compromise was that an up-to-date master list would be made available for consultation at the Home Office.

House of Lords speech: greeted with 'indifference'

On 14 October 1952 anti-vivisection was raised in the House of Lords by Lord Dowding when he appealed for a new inquiry into animal experimentation. Lord Dowding believed that the current law was gravely defi-

Deputation from the Conference of Anti-Vivisection Societies at the Soviet Embassy (Mr Wilfred Tyldesley, Miss Louise Lind-af-Hageby and Dr Beddow-Bayly), 7 January 1958

cient and not properly enforced. He was concerned that the number of experiments taking place was excessive and unduly repetitive, and that the majority were quite irrelevant when applied to humans.

Lord Dowding had been Air Chief Marshal Sir Hugh Dowding, a commanding officer in the Battle of Britain in 1940. He was raised to the peerage in 1943 in recognition of his war service. He believed that Britain should set an example of humanity to other nations by its attitude towards animals and used his place in the House of Lords to further this cause.

He did not call for a Royal Commission but for an 'adequate inquiry' into the entirely new conditions which now existed since the last Royal Commission in 1912. He was personally in favour of the abolition of vivisection but realised it was not practical at present to ask for such legislation. He therefore asked the government to devise a means of enforcing the 1876 Act (there had not been one conviction under the Act in the 76 years since it had come on the statute book), to tighten up the process of granting licences and to take steps to end the indefinite repetition of experiments already made.

His speech was heard with 'indifference' and he did not hear one voice of support from his fellow peers. Following normal parliamentary procedure, he then withdrew his formal motion. BUAV was pleased to note that Lord Dowding was an abolitionist and congratulated him on his 'magnificent speech'. In his preparation he had visited the BUAV office to talk the matter over with the Secretary and had left armed with anti-vivisection literature.

Demonstration against the use of animals in warfare experiments at Porton Down, 25 March 1954

Lord Dowding made a further speech in the House of Lords on 18 July 1957. Once again he made a plea for a new and open inquiry into the present conditions in vivisection laboratories. He gave fresh instances of the defects in the law and drew attention to the secrecy which existed behind the 'closed doors' of the laboratories. He spoke again of humanity and the need for a new way of life based on compassion for all living things. On this occasion he received support from one peer, Lord Somers.

The following year Lord Dowding held a conference at his home. He put forward a scheme which he hoped would make MPs and their political parties take the issue of vivisection more seriously. His aim was to get as many members of the electorate as possible to sign a declaration saying that they would not vote for a parliamentary candidate whose party did not undertake to appoint a statutory commission at the first opportunity to enquire into the working of the law in this country and to amend it in accordance with the findings of the commission. This was aimed not so much at individual MPs but at getting the political parties to act.

Death of Beatrice Kidd: joint 'architect' of the society

Miss Beatrice Kidd, President of BUAV, died on 26 June 1958. She had given over 50 years of service to the society, first appointed as Organising Secretary in 1904, then as Secretary when the Union moved to London in 1905, then as Honorary Secretary, and finally as its President. She gave her last presidential address at the age of 88. Together with Dr Hadwen she had been the 'architect' of the society. They built it up from its modest beginnings into the largest and most active anti-vivisection society in the world.

Miss Kidd had many skills. She was a 'fearless speaker' and made a most formidable opponent on the debating platform. She was a 'clear, concise and forthright' writer and wrote many of the society's pamphlets as well as numerous articles for the journal. She also served as a translator. On her death BUAV recognised that if she had served a more popular cause she might

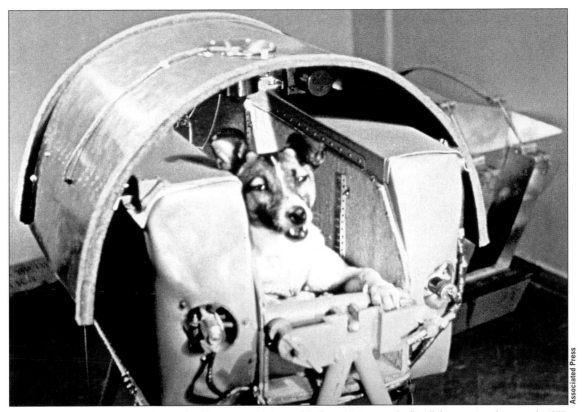

Associated Press

Laika created a storm of protest from animal lovers around the world when she became the first living creature in space in 1957

well have 'reaped high honours' but she would always be honoured in the hearts of those who knew her.

Beatrice Kidd was probably one of the last members of the society to remember the days of Frances Power Cobbe, who was no more than a name from a bygone era for most people. In this respect Miss Kidd's death marked a very definite departure from the past with the society now representing a very different age than when it was first established in 1898. Two days after her death Mr Bruce Elsmere was elected President at the 1958 AGM.

Sacrifice in the space race

The 1950s was the space age - and Russia and the United States became locked in a 'senseless competition' with each other in space research projects. Each country wanted to be the first to land a man on the moon.

On 3 November 1957 a stray dog named Laika, who had been found on the streets of Moscow, became the first living creature in space. She was fired into space inside the satellite Sputnik II amid a cry of rage from animal lovers all round the world. The Russians had announced their intentions some weeks in advance and the Conference of Anti-Vivisection Societies had written at once to the Soviet Embassy in London asking for the project to be called off and for the Ambassador to receive a deputation from the Conference.

A deputation was eventually received at the Soviet Embassy on 7 January 1958. It consisted of Dr Beddow-Bayly, Mr Wilfred Tyldesley and Miss Louise Lind-af-Hageby. The visit received wide publicity in the press and was reported on both television and radio but came too late for Laika.

As well as the terror and suffering which any animal

69

blasted into space would experience, BUAV reminded its supporters of the 'severe suffering' which animals would have been subjected to during months of conditioning before the experiment.

The object of the project was to see what effects space flight would have on the dog's vital organs, and her reactions were transmitted back to earth. Both the Americans and the Russians had extensive space programmes involving the use of live animals. Dogs, monkeys and mice were popular in this type of research. On 3 November 1997 a plaque was unveiled by Russian space scientists in Moscow to mark the 40th anniversary of Laika's journey.

Laboratory demonstrations: a new form of protest

Warfare had provided the basis of an enormous amount of animal experimentation since the First World War. The effects of blast, poison gas, atomic weapons, and deadly chemical and biological poisons were all tested on animals. In Great Britain the animal research establishment at Porton Down was regarded as an 'animal Belsen'.

On 25 March 1954 BUAV organised a demonstration outside Porton Down. Demonstrators representing 30 of the Union's branches met in nearby Salisbury from where they proceeded in coaches, cars and vans to Porton. The police stopped the coaches two miles away and only the smaller vehicles were allowed to carry on. About 70 people managed to get to the entrance to make their protest.

The whole party then returned to Salisbury where the demonstrators marched in procession through the main streets carrying banners and placards and distributing leaflets. The demonstration received wide press publicity.

This demonstration, and one the previous year at the Naval Physiological Laboratory at Alverstoke, Hampshire, marked a new era of demonstrating outside the actual laboratories where vivisection was taking place. These became an increasingly popular form of protest.

CHAPTER 13

The 1960s

A decade of turbulence and controversy - and a new wave of hope

1960s cartoon from *The Anti-Vivisectionist* (**March/ April 1960**)

1960s cartoon from *The Anti-Vivisectionist* (Nov/ Dec 1961)

After a long period of harmony, the 1960s saw BUAV divided in a dispute over policy which had not been so fiercely debated since the turn of the century and which eventually led to an amendment of the Constitution. A government review of the 1876 Act was the first undertaken since the second Royal Commission of 1906/12. Co-operation with other societies was at its most fruitful with a proposed merger between BUAV and NAVS on the agenda again. The changing attitude of the press was apparent with journalists increasingly contacting headquarters for comment and the advent of more sympathetic reporting. BUAV began to see alternatives to animal experiments as a more realistic way of ending animal experiments rather than by legislative change.

New government inquiry triggers BUAV constitutional reform

In 1961 the RSPCA adopted a more radical tone in its campaign against vivisection and on 17 May it sent a deputation with its demands to the Home Secretary, Mr Butler. The RSPCA pointed out the widespread public unease about vivisection, said that it wanted to see reforms in the outdated 1876 Act (including a veterinary presence in the Home Office inspectorate) and suggested that a new advisory committee should be established which included representation from both the veterinary profession and animal protection societies. It transpired that the current advisory committee had met only once during the three years from 1959 to 1961, making its role as 'farcical' as the rest of the machinery of the Act. The demands were far from BUAV's continued call for the abolition of vivisection but nevertheless the two societies retained 'friendly relations'.

The RSPCA undertook a 'forthright' advertising campaign which criticised the 1876 Act for allowing almost unlimited and uncontrollable experiments on animals, and also criticised the Act for not being administered properly. BUAV took the opportunity to echo the words of its great founder, Frances Power Cobbe, who had said that what cannot be controlled must be abolished.

Last-minute preparations in the BUAV committee room at 47 Whitehall before presenting the petition to Parliament, 5 May 1965

BUAV recognised the limitations of the RSPCA's charitable status on its campaigning capacity but thought it had shown a 'great deal of courage' in its efforts.

In November 1962 the new Home Secretary, Henry Brooke, announced that he was setting up a Departmental Committee to examine the workings of the 1876 Act which had governed animal experiments in Great Britain for over 80 years. The composition of the Committee was announced on 23 May 1963 and consisted of 14 names to be chaired by a lawyer, Sir Sydney Littlewood. Although BUAV welcomed this move from the Home Office it was disappointed to discover that the terms of reference of the inquiry were to

consider the present control over experiments on living animals, and to consider whether, and if so what, changes are desirable in the law or its administration.

This left no room for the Committee to include any broader consideration of either the morality or the utility of vivisection. These questions, according to the government, had been addressed by the first two Royal Commissions and it saw no point in returning to them. Vivisection, it seemed, was set to continue no matter what.

This 'bombshell' placed BUAV in an 'insoluble position' as it prevented the organisation from presenting

what it saw as the fundamental arguments against vivisection; these were simply not on the agenda. The Littlewood Committee at its outset was therefore in direct conflict with the aims of the Union. It was to lead to a reawakening of a policy debate which had lain dormant for very many years.

BUAV's policy was one of total abolition. This basic principle had been enshrined in the Constitution of the society and did not allow the Union to support any lesser measure. Furthermore it actually required members of the Executive Committee and holders of any official position to 'oppose any measure of regulation short of prohibition'. Theoretically therefore BUAV should have boycotted the Littlewood inquiry, as it had the second Royal Commission, because it knew that abolition was not on the agenda.

On the other hand, to remain silent seemed almost 'unthinkable' after such a long period without the opportunity to present the Union's voice in a government review. BUAV realised that such a silence might bewilder its members, and lead to misunderstandings. Realistically, it could be many years before such an opportunity came up again.

Deputation from the British Council of Anti-Vivisection Societies delivering the petition to the House of Commons, 5 May 1965, following the publication of the Littlewood Committee report in April

Carrying the petition of over 300,000 signatures into the House of Commons

The matter was given 'long and careful considera-tion' by the Executive Committee. The Littlewood Committee was approached and eventually a way was negotiated for BUAV to contribute evidence without infringing the society's fundamental rule. A compre-hensive 7,000-word Memorandum of Evidence was prepared. Although this made the policy of the society crystal clear, the Memorandum concentrated on show-ing that the Act had totally failed to prevent the suffer-ing of laboratory animals, or even to mitigate suffering to any great extent. This submission was later supple-mented by oral evidence.

At the 1964 AGM a resolution was introduced proposing an amendment to Article 47 of the Constitution. This was intended to release the Executive Committee from its obligation to 'oppose' any measures of partial reform. The resolution was defeated although it was reintroduced at the 1965 AGM and again in 1966 when it was eventually passed. This led to the resignation of some Committee mem-bers, and the President, Mr Gerald Curtler, in protest at what they saw as a departure from the total abolition policy. Mr Jon Evans was elected President in Curtler's place.

Outcome of government inquiry: the Littlewood report

The Littlewood Committee published its report on 29 April 1965. Political interest in the period since the appointment of the Committee had been quiet as most MPs were happy to wait for the findings of the Committee. In order to give political interest a renewed boost, BUAV handed in a petition of over 300,000 sig-natures to the House of Commons the following

The 'foot contingent' of the demonstration against Carworth Europe fronted by BUAV celebrity supporters Celia Hammond and Tania Mallet, 9 June 1966

month. Hundreds of anti-vivisectionists also assembled at the House of Commons to lobby their MPs on a 'memorable occasion' of impressive scale. But when Parliament was dissolved for the forthcoming general election the Littlewood report had not been debated in either House.

Public interest had been stimulated by the Littlewood Committee. In order to take full advantage of this opportunity to promote the anti-vivisection cause BUAV instigated an expensive advertising campaign. Some of the Union's investments had to be sold to meet the costs but the expense was rewarded by a considerable increase in Union membership.

The report of the Littlewood Committee contained 83 recommendations for administrative and other reforms of the 1876 Act but even five years after its presentation to Parliament in 1965 'it has been left to gather dust'.[52] Despite BUAV's efforts the report was never fully debated in Parliament. In general, the recommendations would have increased the level of control over vivisection in Britain, but few were ever implemented. Bearing in mind that this was the first review

of the legislation in such a long time, and that considerable public interest had been aroused,

the Littlewood Report received remarkably little official acknowledgement.[53]

Recommendations 76 to 83 of the Littlewood Committee dealt with the supply of animals to laboratories, an issue which had long been a central BUAV concern. The recommendations suggested the establishment of special breeding centres which would supply laboratory needs.

The new industry for breeding laboratory animals

BUAV had anticipated the development of a new industry for breeding laboratory animals and armed itself for 'vigorous action' against any signs of such an industry evolving. The industry also seemed to anticipate that supply of animals other than by licensed breeders would soon be prohibited and started preparations to take full commercial advantage of the opportunity.

1960s cartoon from *The Anti-Vivisectionist* (July/ August 1961)

1960s cartoon from *The Anti-Vivisectionist* (Sept/ Oct 1962)

There was a notable increase in the number of animal breeding establishments shortly after publication of the Littlewood report. One of these was Britain's first 'animal farm' - Carworth Europe based in Huntingdon, Cambridgeshire.

The Director of Carworth Europe was Dr Lane-Petter, already well known for advocating use of stray cats and dogs in laboratories. This ex-Home Office inspector and ex-Director of the Research Defence Society spoke of the

embarrassing lack of animals in this country for trying out all manner of vital new drugs.[54]

Carworth Europe was a registered company in Britain whose primary purpose was stated as 'breeding of laboratory animals for research organisations, mainly in Europe'. This indicated the company's intention to trade in the export of its animals to laboratories abroad. The commercial interests of the company were apparent and, under current law, all entirely legal. BUAV realised that Carworth Europe wouldn't remain long without 'eager competition'.

In protest against breeding laboratory animals for export, BUAV organised 'perhaps the biggest anti-vivisection demonstration seen in London since World War One'. The demonstration, on 9 June 1966, started early in the morning from outside Carworth Europe in Huntingdon. A motor parade drove down the A1 into London, headed by Public Relations Officer Sidney Hicks towing the BUAV carnival float.

At Speakers' Corner, Marble Arch, the second leg of the demonstration began with the 'foot contingent' headed by celebrity supporter Celia Hammond. The protesters marched down Park Lane, round Hyde Park Corner, down Piccadilly and the Haymarket, round Trafalgar Square and into Whitehall, ending at BUAV headquarters. A deputation also went to 10 Downing Street to hand in a written protest to the Prime Minister against the export of laboratory animals. This was shown on BBC television news.

Rafton Pounder Bill

On 15 November 1966 Mr Rafton Pounder MP introduced a Private Members' Bill to place a total ban on the export of living animals for vivisection research in overseas laboratories. All member societies of the British Council of Anti-Vivisection Societies (formerly the Conference of Anti-Vivisection Societies) campaigned in support of the Bill and wrote to their MPs

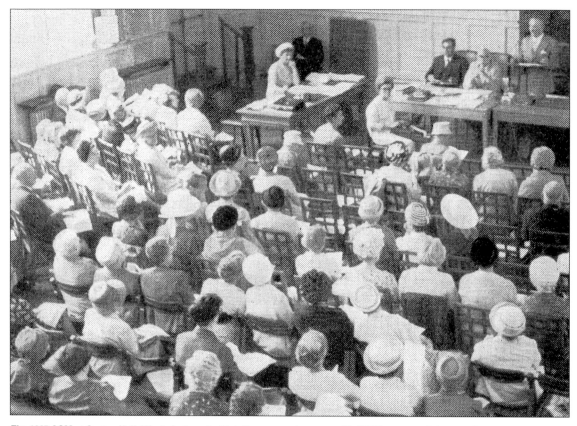

The 1967 AGM at Caxton Hall, Westminster, at which the proposed merger with NAVS was top of the agenda

urging them to support the Bill on VE Day (Vivisection Export Day). In addition the Bill was supported by the RSPCA, the Scottish Society for the Prevention of Cruelty to Animals and the Ulster Society for the Prevention of Cruelty to Animals.

The first reading of the Bill was a success and the second reading was scheduled with 'one foot in the door'. However as the Bill was low down on the list of Private Members' Bills for that session, time ran out and the reading was postponed. Rafton Pounder had to wait until the next parliamentary session to introduce his Bill again. The first reading went unopposed. Once again however parliamentary procedure was against Pounder and at its second reading there were fewer than the requisite number of MPs in the House for it to be passed. The Bill was lost. The only compensation was the publicity it had gained for the cause.

Abortive attempt to amalgamate with NAVS

Jon Evans had been voted in as the new President following the amendment of Article 47 at the 1966 AGM and he re-opened negotiations with NAVS about a possible merger. Discussions were resumed between the executive committees of both societies in an attempt to find a formula for the proposed amalgamation which would be 'mutually acceptable' to both societies.

There was a spirit of optimism which saw the amalgamation leading to the creation of a large and powerful force which would bring a sense of unity and strength hitherto unknown to the anti-vivisection movement. The advantages of amalgamation were clear: better and more economic use of all resources (ending the vast amount of duplication of work by the two societies), the ability to operate on a larger scale, and the presentation of a more effective and united front to both supporters and adversaries. These aims were all 'absolutely desirable' in the best interests of laboratory animals and 'the cause is greater than any one society'. The hope was that working together would bring a speedier end to vivisection. The time was seen as ripe for this amalgamation; it was thought that many people were probably already members of both societies.

The new society was to have a completely new name and a new Memorandum and Articles of Association. A joint statement from NAVS and BUAV was published with the nominations for the holders of office in the new society. Lady Dowding was to be President with Mr John Lefevre as Honorary Treasurer. A Board of Managers of nine was to be chaired by Jon Evans. Plans were taking a very definite shape and the 'deafening' silence from the BUAV membership was taken by its leaders to be a voice of consent.

Ultimately, though, amalgamation was a matter for the members and, at the 'historic' 1967 AGM, BUAV members were asked to vote on the principle of merging with NAVS. However the AGM was to prove that BUAV members had many great concerns over the proposed plans and there was 'considerable apprehension'. There were many objections. In particular there was concern about the way in which members of the new Board of Managers had been selected as it was felt that this was a matter on which the membership should have a say. However after well over two hours of 'solid wrangling' the resolution giving the green light to the proposed merger with NAVS was carried.

Many concerns were raised after the AGM about the actual process of amalgamation. Many thought that a Board of Managers of just nine members would be far too small. The appointment of staff to various posts was the cause of much uneasiness. There were also considerable misgivings over the proposed branch structure and, perhaps most crucially, over the question of the policy of the new society. Whereas NAVS wanted the new society to be committed to a step-by-step approach towards the eventual abolition of vivisection, BUAV still adhered to a policy of abolition without compromise of any kind.

One other issue which was under debate was about support for a Private Members' Bill put forward by Richard Body MP. This Bill proposed the abolition of all exemption certificates available under the 1876 Act.

NAVS was backing the Bill but BUAV regarded it as an 'obvious all time loser' and preferred instead to push for a debate on the Littlewood Committee's report in the forthcoming parliamentary session. BUAV had other reasons not to back Mr Body's Bill. It did not think he was a true anti-vivisectionist and found him quite ignorant of the issues. BUAV therefore could not see how Mr Body could accurately represent the anti-vivisection viewpoint in Parliament. Furthermore, and a matter of great significance, was the discovery that he was in fact a supporter of blood sports. BUAV did not want the anti-vivisection cause 'besmirched' by a connection with someone who advocated such cruel sports.

All too soon it became apparent that there was a 'head on collision' of conflicting fundamental doctrines and, within just four months of the 1967 AGM, amalgamation talks had broken down. At the Executive Committee meeting of 16 November 1967 a resolution was 'reluctantly' passed confirming that amalgamation negotiations had been discontinued.

Jon Evans (President), Reverend Barnard (Vice President) and two members of the Executive Committee resigned over this matter and all four did, in fact, join the NAVS Council of Management. Mr Slatter also resigned as General Secretary and accepted the same post with NAVS. Some BUAV branches disaffiliated themselves because they preferred to join NAVS instead. Reverend AR Eyles was elected as BUAV's new President and Sidney Hicks its new General Secretary.

Alternatives to animal experimentation: the three Rs

The concept of alternatives to animal experiments was first embodied in a publication in 1959 commissioned by UFAW (the Universities Federation for Animal Welfare). Two British scientists, Rex Burch and William Russell, wrote *The Principles of Humane Experimental Techniques* in which they introduced the principle of the three Rs - the reduction, the refinement and the replacement of animals in scientific research.

Also in 1959 a parliamentary question asked whether the government would make a grant for research into alternative methods of discovering remedies for illness. This brought the reply that much research sponsored by the MRC was already devoted to this purpose. BUAV however estimated that only five

1960s campaign literature

per cent of MRC's grant from public funds was devoted to non-vivisectional research.

Increasingly, BUAV began to see promotion of alternatives as a more realistic way to end vivisection, rather than through an Act of Parliament on which it had pinned its hopes for so many years. It was estimated that by using techniques such as tissue culture and computer models over 90 per cent of all current animal experiments could become obsolete. However there was an increasing realisation from the anti-vivisection movement that it would have to take the initiative itself, as successive governments had failed to allocate funds specifically for non-vivisectional medical research.

The Lawson Tait Memorial Trust was founded jointly by BUAV, NAVS and the Scottish Society for the Prevention of Vivisection in 1961. Each society donated £5,000 and elected a trustee. The object of the Trust was to make grants and award prizes for original work of outstanding value to medicine, conducted without the use of live animals and of such a nature that research with living animals in a particular field would be shown to be inexcusable. The founding of the Trust brought widespread publicity and the Trust hoped to set an example for the government to follow.

The Trust was named after a famous 19th century Scottish surgeon, Robert Lawson Tait. Tait had been an anti-vivisectionist and when Dr Hadwen wrote to him for his views on the subject he replied that 'vivisection has done nothing for surgery but lead to horrible bungling', a quote which Hadwen used many times in his debates on the anti-vivisection platform. The Trust was to be an autonomous body, entirely independent from any of the societies which had established it.

The first award of £1,000 from the Trust was made to a surgeon at Whipps Cross Hospital in Walthamstow, London. Shortly afterwards, on 25 September 1964, the official headquarters of the Trust opened in Harley Street, London, and a further grant was announced for two cancer research projects at the University of Edinburgh. In 1965 BUAV made a further donation of £5,000 to the Lawson Tait Memorial Trust noting that it was without doubt 'our greatest weapon in the war against vivisection'.

In 1969 BUAV announced its own plans for a humane research institute which was to be set up in honour of the man who was the 'backbone' of the society for 28 years, Dr Hadwen. This would be a centre where scientists would use non-vivisectional techniques to carry out research into human diseases and to train other scientists in these methods. The proposal was the 'brainchild' of General Secretary, Sidney Hicks. The proposed name of the institute was The Walter Hadwen Foundation and the initial target was to raise £100,000 over a five-year period which would be put into a separate account to establish a charity. Discussions about the institute and fundraising for alternative research methods started in 1970, and led to many important debates on the subject.

BUAV faces a financial crisis

By the end of the 1960s BUAV finances were at 'a dangerously low level'. Expenditure had to be curbed to prevent the possibility of the society folding up. A great deal of money had been spent on projects such as

1960s campaign poster

rebuilding and modernising the front of 47 Whitehall and the purchase of an entire new fleet of vehicles. A major advertising campaign had been initiated at very great expense. At the 1968 AGM the overriding theme was the serious financial position and the depleted state of the Union's resources. Members were warned that the 'spending spree' was over, and that expenditure would have to be slashed and the finances of the society rebuilt. This task was delegated to Mr Guy Herriot, the Honorary Treasurer, whose major concern was that the Union relied far too heavily on legacies, a very unpredictable source of income.

One of the problems was that the branch structure of the Union gave 'pathetically little' financial support to the Union. There was a general feeling that for too long the Union had drifted into a state of administrative apathy with headquarters footing far too much of the bill. It was thought that branches needed to dig deeper into their own funds. With a few exceptions the branches failed to give realistic financial support to headquarters

and, in brutal terms, branches that could not pay their way were described as little more than 'useless limbs'.

At the 1969 AGM a resolution was carried that half of all branch subscriptions should go to headquarters as an affiliation fee. The resolution also required any branch which disaffiliated itself from BUAV to return all branch monies to headquarters within one month of disaffiliation, including the account books and any equipment. Membership fees were raised and it was reluctantly agreed to sell the animal sanctuary in Colchester which had been acquired two years earlier.

By the end of the 1960s BUAV had recovered from its financial crisis and, in the financial year ending March 1970, income exceeded expenditure for the first time since 1964. After the possibility that the Union 'could have died on the amalgamation operating table' the 1969 AGM saw a prevailing spirit of optimism and harmony. A new wave of hope had spread through the Union enabling it to enter the 1970s as a strong and united society.

CHAPTER 14

The 1970s

Heightened political and public awareness of anti-vivisection issues

During the 1970s, as the number of animal experiments carried out in Great Britain peaked, anti-vivisection, and animal rights in general, became high-profile issues. The publication of several key works - by writers such as Richard Ryder, Andrew Linzey and Peter Singer - reawoke the philosophical debate, and the political arena was far from quiet. The centenary of the 1876 Act was acknowledged by Animal Welfare Year and a campaign to 'Put Animals into Politics' was launched. Anti-vivisection issues were increasingly discussed both in the popular press and in scientific journals such as the *British Medical Journal*, *Nature* and *New Scientist*.

There was a succession of presidents through the 1970s following the death of Reverend AR Eyles. Mr Guy Herriot died shortly after election and then Betty Earp held the position from 1972 to 1979. Jean Pink was elected at the 1979 AGM, resigned shortly afterwards and was then re-elected in 1980. At the end of 1976 Sidney Hicks resigned as General Secretary. He had held the post since 1968 and had been a BUAV worker for many years before that. He wished to concentrate on fundraising activities to support the two charities that BUAV had established and which he chaired. He was succeeded by Alan Whittaker.

Exploring alternatives to animal experimentation

When the initial idea for the Dr Hadwen institute was launched the plan had been to build a centre for alternative research. The proposed location was in Gloucester, Dr Hadwen's adopted home town, and the city council had already welcomed intentions to purchase land to build such a centre. Professor Aygun, one of the leading cell and tissue culture pioneers, was appointed as scientific adviser and offered to train a scientist appointed by the Trust at his own research establishment in Ankara, Turkey.

The Dr Hadwen Trust for Humane Research was

Mrs Betty Earp, BUAV President 1972 to 1979

registered as a charity in 1970 to raise funds for building the institute and in order to develop as an independent organisation. In the meantime the Trust offered sponsorship to postgraduate students who were training in non-animal research techniques. By 1973 however plans to build a research institute were put on hold, partly because of the huge amount of money needed, but also because it appeared that scientists preferred to work in existing, established laboratories. The trustees therefore decided to concentrate on raising funds to combat three major diseases: arthritis, cancer and diabetes. The money raised was used to make grants to scientists working on non-vivisectional techniques to research into these diseases, and to buy essential equipment for their research work.

One individual, Jack Malone, set out to walk 3,000 miles round Great Britain in eight months and to raise £10,000 for the Trust under the slogan 'Hobo for Humanity'. Although

In the 1970s BUAV established two independent charities to further its work

Jack was unable to finish the whole distance he did an extremely important job as an ambassador for the cause by raising the profile of the Trust. He met the lord mayors of the towns he visited and held numerous press, radio and television interviews.

In support of the charity it had established one of BUAV's key campaigns throughout the 1970s was to try and persuade the government to allocate a specific amount from its huge annual medical research grant, for research using non-vivisection techniques. BUAV did not want to appear to be opposed to all medical research, only that which involved living animals. Young scientists had expressed a willingness to turn to these new types of research if the necessary funds and equipment were available. A Bill was introduced to ban the use of animals where alternative research methods were available - but failed.

The government made its first financial support to the development of alternatives in 1984 when it awarded grants to FRAME, the Fund for the Replacement of Animals in Medical Experiments (£185,000), and to the Universities Fund for Animal Welfare (£30,000).

Raising awareness about cosmetic testing

The use of animals to test cosmetic products was first brought to public attention in the 1970s. In October 1973 BUAV conducted a survey of 500 people in London and concluded that there was a lot of work to be done to combat ignorance on this issue. It began an intensive campaign in 1974. In the same year the RSPCA commissioned a national opinion poll on the subject which concluded that a large majority of the public disapproved of the practice.

Christmas 1974 saw shoppers in London's Oxford Street targeted by BUAV and encouraged to buy cruelty-free Christmas presents. An earlier survey of 200 young women had indicated by an overwhelming majority that they would not continue to use make-up if they thought animals had suffered in the industry and that they were satisfied with the choice of products already on the market.

Massive public uproar over smoking beagles

In February 1975 the *Sunday People* newspaper exposed the story of beagles being forced to smoke tobacco in an experiment at Imperial Chemical Industries (ICI) laboratories in Cheshire. BUAV reported in its newspaper that 'never before in the entire history of the British Union has there been such an uproar against the use of live animals in experimentation'[55] as over this story. The impact was highlighted by the use of explicit and emotive photographs which shocked the nation. It caused outrage among many people who hadn't previously protested against vivisection and there was a public awakening about just how widespread vivisection had become.

BUAV presented a petition of 130,000 signatures to the House of Commons, along with details of alternative experimental techniques, and Lord Houghton introduced a Private Members' Bill into the House of Lords to outlaw this type of research. Although the Bill was not successful the Home Secretary did announce that

Mirror Syndication International

This picture of beagles forced to inhale tobacco smoke, first published in 1975, shocked the nation and introduced many people to the issue of vivisection for the first time

after the end of ICI's experiment, dogs would not be used again in smoking research in Britain.

Continued campaigning for new legislation

BUAV had long argued that the 1876 Act was hopelessly out of date and, in 1976, the centenary of the Act, its campaign about the need for new legislation was intensified.

Criticisms about the 1876 Act were numerous. BUAV had always protested that the very practices which the Union's founders had set out to prohibit could be overcome if exemption certificates were granted. For example, Certificate A, which allowed anaesthesia to be dispensed with, was used in more than 80 per cent of all experiments. There had not been one single conviction under the Act in 100 years despite numerous infringements recorded in the Home Office annual returns. Offenders were usually admon-

ished or, in extreme cases, had their personal licence to experiment revoked. No member of the public was ever allowed into a laboratory, nor indeed was an RSPCA inspector.

In 1876 there were 350 experiments recorded by the Home Office, in contrast to over 5 million recorded in 1976. BUAV argued that the Act belonged to a bygone age when animal experimentation was not only carried out on a different scale, but was also of a different nature. By the 1970s, over 50 per cent of experiments were being conducted for commercial interests - not for medical research. This was highlighted by the publication of Richard Ryder's book *Victims of Science* in 1975 which drew attention to the widespread trivial and commercial uses of laboratory animals. There was increasing frustration at the government's refusal to promote alternative methods of research.

A new Home Secretary, Merlyn Rees, was appoint-

BUAV supported the work of Lord Houghton (left) and Clive Hollands to 'Put Animals into Politics'

ed in 1976. BUAV wrote to him immediately urging him to 'be a crusader' and replace the 1876 Act with humane legislation which reflected the advances made in medical research since 1876. BUAV also launched its 'Scrap the Act' campaign and distributed 100,000 protest kits.

In 1976 BUAV replaced its newspaper *AV Times* with a new journal called *Animal Welfare*. This was the journal of BUAV and its two recently-established charities, the Dr Hadwen Trust for Humane Research and the Animal Welfare Trust. Two special editions of *Animal Welfare* were produced for Animal Welfare Year.

Animal Welfare Year

August 1976 to August 1977 was designated Animal Welfare Year in recognition of the centenary of the 1876 Act. Animal Welfare Year was a national campaign involving nearly 70 animal welfare societies. The campaign focused on prevention of cruelty and promotion of humanity in four key areas of animal welfare issues: pet animals, farm animals, wild animals and laboratory animals. The campaign registered itself as a company. Lord Houghton was its President and the Chairman was Clive Hollands of the Scottish Society for the Prevention of Vivisection.

Animal Welfare Year was primarily a publicity cam-

paign. It was regarded by its organisers as the greatest opportunity ever presented to animal welfare societies to put their message across to the public, the press and Parliament. Lord Houghton was keen to cultivate a spirit of co-operation and encouraged the societies to sink their differences and work towards the common goal of the protection of animals.

Private Members' Bills keep the debate alive

The need for legislative reform was reflected in the number of Private Members' Bills introduced throughout the late 1960s and during the 1970s. In 1979 two more were introduced into Parliament dealing with reform of the 1876 Act. One was presented into the House of Lords by Lord Halsbury, President of the RDS, and one was presented into the House of Commons by Peter Fry and backed by the RSPCA. The Executive Committee declared its complete opposition to Halsbury's Bill and while Fry's was more acceptable it was considered by BUAV to have some very serious failings. Neither Bill was nearly as radical as BUAV would have liked, but it took advantage of the opportunity provided by the debate to push for its own goals.

Fry's Bill did reach a second reading but then 'foundered in the quagmires that lie in wait for any Private Member's Bill'.[56] Halsbury's Bill reached the committee stage and although it never became law it did lead to a thorough investigation by a House of Lords select committee.

Campaign to 'Put Animals into Politics'

The message to politicians and the general public of the General Election Co-ordinating Campaign for Animal Protection, established in 1978, was to 'Put Animals into Politics'. Lord Houghton (Chairman) and Clive Hollands (Secretary) wanted to convince MPs and the electorate that animal welfare was a political issue: it wanted the government to accept responsibility for animal issues. It was a generally accepted notion that it was no longer satisfactory to leave this important issue to Private Members' Bills but needed government debate and government action.

In the run-up to the 1979 general election, prospective parliamentary candidates were lobbied for their opinion on a variety of animal issues and the public were encouraged to use their vote on behalf of ani-

Cartoon from BUAV publicity materials, 1960s/1970s

mals. In the face of growing public concern over a number of issues - including animal experimentation, cruel sports and factory farming - political parties were encouraged to adopt a party policy. The 1979 general election was the first time that all three major political parties included animal welfare in their manifestos.

The new Conservative government, which came to power in 1979 under Margaret Thatcher, had made a pre-election promise to reform the 1876 Act. The Committee for the Reform of Animal Experimentation submitted proposals to the Home Secretary in November 1979 for a new law governing animal experimentation. The principle behind its proposed Act was that animals should only be used in 'justifiable medical research'. It also addressed areas of concern such as a reduction in the number of animals used, the restriction of pain, the development of alternatives and public accountability. The Committee urged the government to come as close as possible to these proposals when framing new legislation, and also to allow room for a progressive tightening-up and restriction on the use of animals in research. The government was not to act on this issue for several more years but, when it did, CRAE became an official advisory body in alliance with FRAME and the British Veterinary Association.

A new home

In 1977 BUAV began to look for a new home and an appeal fund for the new headquarters was launched. This was hurried along by the news that 47 Whitehall was to be demolished and rebuilt and, in July 1979, BUAV headquarters moved to a temporary new home at 143 Charing Cross Road where it was to stay for four years.

There was an increasing feeling emerging at headquarters that the system of branches had become outdated. In the early days, the branches had done valuable work bringing the anti-vivisection message to the people. They had retained a high degree of independence and raised their own money which they could spend as they wished. There was criticism that the branches still clung to this autonomy and did not always conform to the Union's Articles of Association. The branch structure was clearly in decline. In 1970 there were still approximately 100 branches but by 1980 they numbered just 20.

For branches without a secretary, chairman or committee members it was decided that all branch accounts, documentation and membership records would be transferred to headquarters until new staff could be found. In practice, more often than not, a branch was not re-established once it had become redundant. However, the branch structure would not be formally disbanded until the 1990s.

CHAPTER 15

The 1980s

Achieving a political voice: BUAV reinvents itself as an effective lobbying force

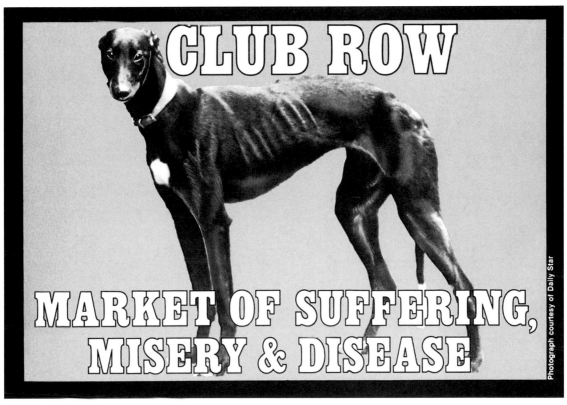

Material from the campaign to close down Club Row animal market, early 1980s

By the beginning of the 1980s BUAV was 'in a state of civil war'. In-fighting was the order of the day. The 1970s had done much to promote animal rights issues and this had led to an influx of a newer and younger generation of members. These 'young Turks' were much dissatisfied with the present state of BUAV and a battle for power, waged since the 1979 AGM, was eventually won by the younger generation. They were themselves to be replaced five years later by yet another faction, following another internal dispute.

By the end of the 1980s the society had become a more professional organisation, and had achieved a political voice and increased credibility.

The early 1980s, and the 'old guard' versus the 'young Turks'

The problems surrounding the 'turbulent and unhappy period' between 1979 and 1981 were based on two issues. Firstly, there had been some concern about certain BUAV financial dealings coupled with a sense that the society was too entrenched in the past and placed far too great an emphasis on the rehoming of animals

New hard-hitting images reflected the new style of the organisation in the early 1980s

and far too little on fighting vivisection. Secondly, the tone of the Union was felt to be too moderate and passive as reflected in the title of the society's journal *Animal Welfare*. Propaganda materials were thought to lack impact: there were reports that one member of staff criticised them for being 'too flabby to dent the skin of a well constructed rice pudding'.

By the end of 1981 BUAV had almost an entirely new staff - fronted by Margaret Manzoni (Office Manager) and Kim Stallwood (Campaigns Officer) - and

a new Executive Committee. The 'old guard' were out and the young Turks were in. Under the new leadership new and more daring campaigns were undertaken. A membership recruitment drive was undertaken which included advertising on the London Underground. New hard-hitting propaganda materials were produced and the first edition of a new-style journal, *The Liberator*, appeared in September 1981. After the resignation of Jean Pink, Richard Ryder was elected as the new, and what would be the last, BUAV President in 1981. The

Weekly demostrations were held at Club Row animal market in the early 1980s

posts of president and vice president were abolished at the 1983 AGM as they were considered 'outdated' and not in keeping with the new radical image of the society.

In 1983 BUAV moved from its temporary home at 143 Charing Cross Road to a new and permanent home at 16a Crane Grove in the London borough of Islington. This was considered an appropriate site as Islington had been the first council to adopt an Animals Rights Charter in 1982.

Grass roots campaigning

The once flourishing network of BUAV branches now stood at less than 20. They were being replaced by local animal rights groups which were springing up across the country. These groups campaigned on all animal rights issues and, unlike the branches, which were expected to be loyal to the Union, would ally themselves to any national group offering them support. As the membership of BUAV 'soared' many of these new recruits also became members of a local group. Local groups therefore had to be organised into an effective campaigning force for the benefit of BUAV.

A system of contacts was established which could mobilise the membership into an effective grass roots campaign at a local level. A 'contact' (who was expected to be a member) acted as a link between BUAV and a local animal rights group. He or she would promote BUAV's work in their area and organise local activities in support of campaigns initiated by headquarters. The members of BUAV saw themselves not just as members of a particular society but part of a much wider movement.

Club Row: the 'market of misery'

Club Row was an animal market in London's East End which was dubbed the 'market of misery'. Every Sunday morning animals were traded here, both legally and illegally, like something out of a 'Dickensian novel'. The animals sold at the market could easily end up in a laboratory and those which could not be sold were often simply dumped onto the street at the end of the day.

The market became a focus for animal rights campaigners. BUAV adopted the campaign initiated by Co-ordinating Animal Welfare (CAW) which aimed to close down Club Row and every market of its kind in the country. The campaign was backed by Lord Houghton who sought to pass an amendment to the Pet Animals Act 1951 to end the street trading of animals altogether. This was eventually passed on 9 May 1983.

Sunday morning traders had to face weekly demonstrations from protesters who were kept in check by a

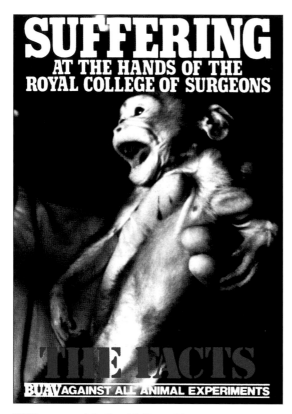

BUAV prosecuted the Royal College of Surgeons for its treatment of a laboratory monkey, Mone, in February 1985

regular police presence. The traders even complained to the local council, Tower Hamlets, about noise pollution from the demonstrators. However on 24 November 1982 the Consumer and Social Services Committee of Tower Hamlets council voted to stop all trading of live animals from market stalls in the borough from 1 July 1983 and this decision was ratified by its full council on 16 December 1983. A small, but important battle had been won.

Telling the truth about what went on in laboratories

As the Union became flooded with younger, more active members it had to address the question of how to tackle issues being raised by animal liberationists, most popularised by the Animal Liberation Front (ALF). Although BUAV was not itself responsible for organis-

ing any raids on laboratories, it clearly sympathised with the activities of those frustrated by the political process who were determined to take a more active role. This was reflected in the pages of *The Liberator* which regularly reported acts of liberation.

BUAV went further than this, however. It used evidence obtained during raids to publicise the cause and to tell the truth about what went on in British laboratories. The most notable example of this was when BUAV decided to bring a prosecution against the Royal College of Surgeons of England (RCS). This followed a raid on its laboratory in Downe, Kent, in August 1984 by the South East Animal Liberation League (SEALL).

The case focused on Mone, a 10-year-old female breeding macaque monkey. Documents obtained in the raid revealed how in June 1984 she had been found collapsed and in a severely dehydrated state, and had needed a fluid intravenous drip to recover. This occurred just four days after a visit from a Home Office inspector. Many of the other monkeys were also in a poor condition and suffered from cuts caused by the poor state of their caging.

BUAV prepared a detailed report on the suffering of the monkeys at the College and brought about a private prosecution against the Royal College of Surgeons under the Protection of Animals Act 1911. This Act, which eventually superseded Martin's Act, was intended to protect animals from cruelty and unnecessary suffering. After a seven-day hearing RCS was found guilty at Bromley magistrates' court in February 1985 of 'wantonly and unreasonably causing unnecessary suffering' to Mone. This was the first time that a professional body such as the RCS had been convicted of such a charge.

The College's appeal in July 1985 was dismissed but then in January 1986 the conviction was quashed on the basis of a legal technicality. BUAV had served a further 10 summonses on RCS relating to its care of other monkeys in the laboratory but had decided not to pursue these as it could have ended up a costly affair. Much adverse publicity against the College had already been achieved which would have 'marred their image for all time'.

BUAV launched a nationwide campaign in November 1985 to free Mone as she had not actually been rescued during the raid. Local publicity stunts were organised across the country and, on 1 February

Demonstrators at World Day for Laboratory Animals, Salisbury, 1982

1986, 1,000 demonstrators marched through Downe. They handed a letter into the College requesting the release of Mone, along with a giant key to symbolise freedom. The greatest tragedy of the whole affair was that despite all the adverse publicity and court cases Mone was still there. The College considered BUAV's campaign to be 'ill-conceived' and had no intention of transferring Mone to its care.

World Day for Laboratory Animals

By the 1980s the coalitions to which BUAV had once belonged had been disbanded. World Day for Laboratory Animals however represented an act of co-operation among the main anti-vivisection groups, and national demonstrations were staged every year in a show of solidarity within the animal rights movement. Each year focused on a different theme. In 1982, when

Britain was at war with Argentina over the Falkland Islands, military research at Porton Down was the focus with a procession led by people dressed in germ warfare suits and gas masks. In 1983 the research laboratories of the British Industrial Biological Research Association (BIBRA) and the MRC at Carshalton were the focal points, and Wickham Laboratories in 1985. In 1986 psychology experiments were the key issue with demonstrations taking place at Swansea, Cambridge and Manchester universities.

'Mobilisation for Laboratory Animals': against the government's proposals

The Conservative government which came to power in 1979 had made a pre-election promise to update legislation on animal experimentation, but did not act immediately as it claimed to be waiting for the Council of

During the 1980s it was estimated that an animal died in a British laboratory every six seconds

Europe to conclude its deliberations on this matter. Eventually the government published its White Paper *Scientific Procedures on Living Animals* on 12 May 1983. But anti-vivisectionists were far from impressed: they argued that any legislation based on this paper would offer little protection to laboratory animals. They regarded the white paper as an attempt to convince the public in the run-up to the next election that the government had the interests of laboratory animals in mind. In reality the proposals would merely maintain the status quo. The new legislation might be given a new name but it would in effect be the same 'Victorian legislation' that was already on the statute books.

In response, the four major anti-vivisection societies of Britain - BUAV, NAVS, Animal Aid and the Scottish Anti-Vivisection Society - joined forces in a coalition under the campaigning banner 'Mobilisation for

Laboratory Animals: Against the Government's Proposals'. Their intention was to make sure that legislation did not reach the statute books framed on the white paper.

The Mobilisation campaign had six minimum demands that it wanted to see incorporated into any legislation. These demands were a ban on experiments in the following areas: cosmetics, tobacco and alcohol, the Draize eye test (in which a test substance is dripped into the eye of a rabbit and the effect monitored), the LD50 test (a crude toxicity test in which a group of animals is poisoned in order to find the dose of a test substance necessary to kill 50 per cent of the animals used), warfare experiments, and all behavioural and psychological experiments. The campaign also called for the exclusion from the Home Office Advisory Committee of those with a 'vested interest' in the continuation of animal experiments. Briefing papers and scientific critiques were produced which provided scientifically accurate arguments against the areas of experimentation it wished to see banned.

A week of action took place in May 1984 culminating in a national march and rally in Trafalgar Square. It was a protest of 'peace, solidarity and determination' attended by an estimated 9,000 people. In a dramatic visual representation of the toll of death in British laboratories a bell was sounded 'every six seconds' at which point another person was snatched from the crowd by blood splattered scientists until 600 'victims' lay dead on the ground of Trafalgar Square.

In May 1985 the government published a second white paper but the proposals were still 'totally unacceptable' to anti-vivisectionists as not one single area of experimentation was to be banned.

A commitment was made to introduce a Bill in the Queen's speech of 6 November 1985 and, almost immediately, the Animals (Scientific Procedures) Bill was introduced into the House of Lords. The Bill was based on the recommendations of the second white paper. It is often the case that legislation is introduced into the Lords first when the government anticipates controversy. It passed through the Lords and had its first reading in the House of Commons in February 1986 with the final reading set for May. The Mobilisation leaders met with many sympathetic MPs and peers during this period and organised a highly successful lobby of Parliament in February 1986, attended

BUAV protested outside the Houses of Parliament as the Animals (Scientific Procedures) Act 1986 became law

by over 700 people.

The Bill received Royal assent on 20 May 1986 and was to be fully implemented over a two-year period. The passing of the Animals (Scientific Procedures) Act 1986 brought the Mobilisation campaign to an end. Three years of intense campaigning from the leading national societies and thousands of supporters had failed to stop the legislation or to extract even a single concession. All minimum demands had been ignored. BUAV began to realise that political lobbying needed to become an essential component of any future campaigning strategy.

Internal disputes resurface

BUAV underwent another 'internal dispute' during the passage of the 1986 Act. This was the result of a long-standing disagreement within the Executive Committee about management, policy and direction of the society. Another series of changes in 1985 left both the staff and Executive Committee transformed. Internal disputes did nothing to help the cause which the Union represented: they only led to a series of financial implications. Far more costly was the damage to morale and to the effectiveness of campaigns.

An emergency general meeting (EGM) was convened in June 1985 by those who supported an internal review of the organisation. They wanted to see an investment in the future, and the development of a more professional and positive approach to campaigning. They used provisions within the Companies Act to convene a meeting at which a motion of no confidence in certain members of the Executive Committee was passed.

BUAV dissociates itself from violent action

As an increasingly hostile media portrayed animal rights campaigners as 'fanatics' and 'terrorists', BUAV set out to create a new beginning and relaunch itself. A further EGM was called in November 1985 in an attempt to define BUAV policy on direct action more clearly. BUAV understood people's frustration at the continuing suffering of animals as a result of the intransigence shown by successive governments. At the same time it would not condone acts of physical violence committed in the name of animal rights. This clarification of policy marked a new approach to the campaigning style of the organisation.

Political role: stark choices needed

Following the passing of the 1986 Act BUAV deliberately maintained a low political profile for the next three years during which time it had to face 'a stark choice'. The organisation had been excluded from any negotiations about the Bill on the grounds of its alleged support for illegitimate and illegal activities. BUAV realised that it would have to establish itself as an effective lobbying force or, in effect, continue to be ruled out of any future political debate.

Cosmetic campaign: 'Choose Cruelty-free'

Immediately following the passing of the 1986 Act, BUAV not only maintained a low political profile, it also halted its campaigning activities. BUAV was not however stagnating: it was planning the launch of a major new campaign. In March 1987, after a year of intensive preparation, a new campaign was launched called

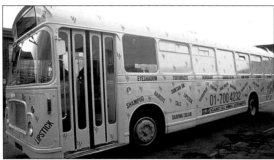

Left: The 'Choose Cruelty-free' bus which toured England was later refurbished for the 'Health with Humanity' campaign

Above: The launch of the "Choose Cruelty-free' campaign was supported by a nationwide advertising campaign, 1987

'Choose Cruelty-free'. The campaign, headed by Campaigns Organiser Steve McIvor, centred on the continued use of animals in cosmetic experiments and represented a new approach to campaigning.

The campaign moved away from the radical style that had been associated with BUAV since the early 1980s and attempted instead to take a more positive approach *and* retain a powerful message. The emphasis was on promoting cruelty-free products rather than the commonly-used tactic of boycotting certain products. The campaign had the backing of a number of companies including The Body Shop.

A huge drive was launched to raise public awareness. Adverts were placed in consumer magazines, posters were displayed at bus shelters and in shopping centres, displays were held in schools and libraries, leaflets were placed in retail outlets and a telephone hotline was set up to deal with the influx of enquiries. An information pack was sent out in response to the thousands of enquiries received at the office each week.

A single decker bus was bought which was specially converted into a 'mobile information centre' and painted in the campaign colours. A national bus tour was undertaken which was to take the message right across the country.

From the outset the campaign was intended to be a long-term activity. It was recognised that it could take several years for cosmetic tests to be ended in this country, and even longer worldwide. But it represented 'a barrier that must be crossed if further, more radical progress is to be made'. A ban on cosmetic testing did not need any legislative intervention: it could be achieved under the existing 1986 Act.

After raising public awareness, and encouraging commercial interest, the next phase was to get more cruelty-free products onto the shelves of major supermarkets, chemists and department stores. Retailers and manufacturers were encouraged to respond to increasing consumer demand for cosmetics which had not been tested on animals. One of the long-term strategies of the campaign was that thousands of people would be introduced to the anti-vivisection issue for the first time.

A questionnaire was devised which provided the basis for assessing whether or not a product was cruelty-free. Producing cruelty-free criteria was an area fraught with difficulty but the issues had to be tackled.

All those companies which met the criteria were 'approved' and promoted in BUAV's *Approved Product Guide* which became an enormous success and in great demand. The guide had to be revised annually to keep up to date with the increasing number of companies joining the campaign. All approved companies were also eligible to use the white rabbit logo on their products - a registered trademark which confirmed that a company had met the BUAV criteria.

'Health with Humanity': campaign against use of animals in medical research

The 'Health with Humanity' campaign followed the cosmetic campaign, and was launched in June 1988. This tackled the highly emotive and controversial issue of the use of animals in medical research. It was designed as an educational campaign because although the majority of people were opposed to cosmetic experiments, public opinion generally, albeit cautiously, accepted medical research as an unfortunate necessity. The central theme of the campaign was the message that 'animal experiments tell us about animals and not about people'. Once again the campaign was researched extensively and the arguments presented in a positive and professional way. An educational video narrated by BBC presenter Sue Cook was also produced which concentrated on demonstrating the arguments instead of showing gory images.

The first phase of the campaign targeted universities where medical research was being conducted. The 'Choose Cruelty-free' campaign bus was refitted and a national tour was again used to take the message to the targeted institutions. The campaign received excellent local media coverage.

The second phase of the campaign was launched in 1990 under the campaigning slogan 'Where Charity Ends'. The campaign exposed the 'cruel contradiction' of how the public often unwittingly funded animal research through charitable donations. Medical research charities which funded research involving animal experiments were targeted and a guide was produced to enable the public to make a positive choice when donating to charities to ensure their money could not end up funding such experiments. The impact of this campaign was demonstrated in the establishment of a coalition of medical research charities the following year. The Research for Health Charities Group aimed to

'Health with Humanity' campaign image, 1988

promote greater public awareness of the role of animals in medical research.

Undercover investigation: exposing realities behind closed doors

Information about what took place in British laboratories had always been restricted. In the 1980s, because of increasing fears over direct action, the Home Office even restricted the distribution of the list of premises registered under the 1876 Act which had always been available previously. As BUAV had conscientiously moved away from using evidence obtained during illegal raids, it turned instead to undercover investigations. These became a highly successful technique for acquiring otherwise unobtainable information, and exposed the realities of what went on behind closed doors. Undercover investigations were carried out lawfully usually by someone taking a job in a laboratory.

In 1989 BUAV was able to expose the truth behind the fate of ex-racing greyhounds which were being sold for vivisection by a Welsh company called Denisu Supplies. The dogs were being handed over to a man, who then sold them to Denisu, by the NGRC's own rehoming scheme, the Retired Greyhound Trust.

A fictitious company was established by BUAV which arranged to buy six of these greyhounds from Denisu saying they were for a French research laboratory. The deal was set up for 23 March 1989 and the dogs were delivered to an air freight company near Heathrow Airport, supposedly for export. The dogs could be identified through their tattoo markings, and five of the six dogs could be traced as registered racing dogs.

A seven-month investigation uncovered the chain of supply by which the greyhounds passed from unsuspecting owners to research laboratories. Denisu Supplies was central to this chain. The story obtained national media coverage and BUAV called on the Home Office not to grant Denisu a licence as a laboratory supplier. Although the Home Office failed to take any action Denisu Supplies closed down shortly after the exposé. The NGRC acted positively and implemented a new rule to tighten up the procedures for its rehoming scheme. It announced that owners would be banned from racing for life if they broke the rules. The rescued dogs were all safely rehomed.

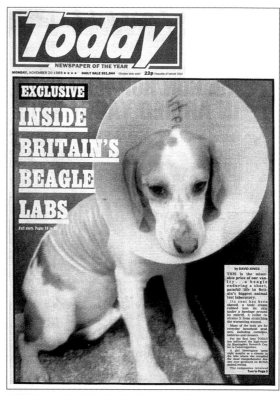

BUAV's exposé of Huntingdon Research Centre made headline news in November 1989

Huntingdon Research Centre: everyday suffering at a 'centre of excellence'

In 1989 Sarah Kite worked for eight months as a BUAV undercover investigator at Huntingdon Research Centre (HRC), Europe's largest commercial contract testing laboratory. Her job as a weekend worker involved cleaning, feeding and watering the animals, first in the rodent and then in the dog toxicology unit. Sarah kept a diary in which she noted down details of the testing that she witnessed, the companies that were sponsoring research and the level of animal suffering involved. Later she also smuggled in a camera to get photographic evidence which would appear on the front of *Today* newspaper when the story was finally exposed in November 1989.

BUAV compiled a detailed dossier of the investigation. This was to provide 'a damning insight' into the everyday suffering of animals in a laboratory which pro-

moted itself as a 'centre of excellence'. The story received intense media coverage, particularly in the Huntingdon area. The Managing Director of HRC refused to meet with BUAV to discuss the findings, preferring to 'wait for the dust to settle'. No meeting ever took place. Local animal rights groups took up the campaign and held a series of pickets outside HRC. BUAV arranged public meetings in Huntingdon and a new leaflet, *Secret Suffering*, was widely distributed.

BUAV called on the Home Office to conduct a full inquiry based on the investigation, and questions were asked in Parliament. The point of the investigation had been to expose the everyday suffering of animals in British laboratories sanctioned under the Animals (Scientific Procedures) Act 1986. Although the Home Office failed to act on this occasion they could not so easily ignore the evidence obtained on video during a further undercover investigation in 1997.

CHAPTER 16

The 1990s

BUAV comes of age: a century of campaigning against cruelty

By the 1990s BUAV had trans formed itself into a modern, professional and effective pressure group with an established voice in the political arena, both at British and European levels. Following yet another internal conflict in 1994 it undertook a number of measures to try and resolve once and for all the periodic infighting that it had been subject to. It continued its campaigning activities in a positive and professional manner and, through the establishment of the European Coalition to End Cosmetic Tests On Animals, it set into motion the means by which high-profile campaigns could be carried right across Europe. The latest of the society's journals, *Campaign Report*, was introduced in 1991 replacing *The Liberator*.

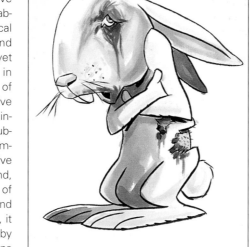
Artist's sketch of Vanity

The 'moderates' versus the 'radicals'

The most recent case of dissension within the ranks happened in 1994 when a dispute over policy and tactics split both the Executive Committee and the staff into two clear camps. The existing regime was criticised by various factions who were unhappy with the developments that had taken place since the late 1980s when there had been a strong move towards professionalism and more achievable campaign targets. Some of the critics felt that BUAV should support direct action; others felt that it should be concentrating on the 'harder' medical issues; yet others felt that not enough support was given to local activists in the campaign strategy.

An attempt to oust the professional wing of BUAV at the 1994 AGM plunged the society into crisis when a divided Executive Committee was elected. Six members from each faction were returned. This stifled the campaigning capacity of the organisation as all attention was focused on resolving the dispute. Proxy voting, which gave all members a chance to vote on issues at AGMs without actually being present, was seen as a means of addressing these problems but this, in itself, then became the central issue of the dispute.

The 'radicals' argued that opposition to proxy voting had been written into the original Constitution of the Union and that any departure from this 'would mark the death knell of the BUAV'. The radicals argued that proxy voting was open to abuse and its introduction would enable those in power to become less accountable to activists. They thought that attendance at AGMs was essential and only members who had shown the commitment to attend and participate in a full debate should be entitled to vote.

The 'moderates' on the other hand saw proxy voting as a way of making the organisation more democratic. The moderates argued that many members were simply unable to attend meetings, especially those who lived outside London. They stated that the Constitution had been drafted when membership was much smaller and largely London-based. As only a small proportion of members attended AGMs it made the organisation susceptible to take-over bids by minority factions.

Vanity and her European cousins in Strasbourg, 1992

The moderate element called for an EGM in an attempt to appeal to all BUAV members and to discuss the issue of proxy voting. The radicals tried, but failed, to get a court injunction banning the event (they had themselves made an invalid requisition for an EGM) and banning BUAV from republishing material which the six claimed defamed them. The main items for discussion at the EGM were the future of the six dissenting committee members and the introduction of proxy voting. The meeting, which was attended by about 800 members, had to be ended by the police following severe disruption from the radical element.

In order to break the deadlock, the moderates took legal action and, in February 1995, after months of difficulty at BUAV, a High Court judge ruled in favour of allowing the BUAV membership to vote, by post, on the issue of proxy voting and on the future membership of the Executive Committee. The judge accepted that it was impractical to hold another EGM, given the likelihood of further disruption, and so allowed BUAV to conduct a postal vote in an effort to try and resolve the situation. The results of the election indicated an overwhelmingly majority (78 per cent) of members were in favour of the introduction of proxy voting and returned the moderate members of the Executive Committee, including two members who had been co-opted in the interim period. Only one member of the radical faction was returned.

The AGM in 1995 was the first to incorporate the results of proxy voting and BUAV was able to return its full attention to campaigning. In the hope of putting such internal problems behind it once and for all, BUAV decided to carry out a thorough review of its Constitution which had been central to the recent upheaval. The proposals put forward were carried at the 1996 AGM leaving BUAV with a revised, modern and more stable Constitution. The network of branches, which had fallen into decline, was formally dissolved leaving the society operating solely from its London headquarters. The society had clearly broken from the remnants of the mid-1980s and established its position as a professional campaigning organisation.

'Cosmetic Testing: It's In Your Hands'

The cosmetic campaign continued into the 1990s and a hard-hitting cinema advertisement was released. A campaign mascot, designed and produced by the creators of *Spitting Image* puppets, was adopted. Vanity, the-larger-than-life laboratory rabbit, was introduced to the media at a press conference in February 1991 and has been a regular favourite at BUAV publicity events ever since. Four mascots were produced, one to work in Britain and three to work on the continent.

In 1992 the European Parliament had voted overwhelmingly in favour of an effective ban on the marketing of cosmetics tested on animals from 1 January 1998. In response to news that this ban was to be postponed, perhaps indefinitely, BUAV launched its own campaign in June 1997 - 'Cosmetic Testing: It's In Your Hands' - in order to bring about an end to cosmetic testing by voluntary means.

A new international standard was drawn up which was adopted by over 50 animal protection groups across Europe and in the United States. The standard was designed to act as internationally recognised criteria for what constituted a cosmetic or toiletry product which was not tested on animals. The standard was launched simultaneously in London, Brussels and the United States giving it a truly international status. Over 140 companies signed up to the standard pledging to put into place all the required systems by January 1998, the date from which the proposed ban would have taken effect. A national advertising campaign was launched attracting extensive media coverage.

For many years BUAV had been at the forefront of pushing for an end to cosmetic testing. In 1997 it welcomed the announcement from the Home Secretary of a ban on the future testing of all finished cosmetic products. Although this measure was seen as a significant step in the right direction, BUAV pledged to continue to campaign for a ban on the testing of cosmetic ingredients too.

International trade in primates

Another issue that had been close to BUAV's heart was that of primates, both their continued use in experiments and the appalling trade by which they were supplied to laboratories. In 1992 BUAV launched a high-profile media campaign called 'Paradise Lost' which, for the first time, exposed the grim reality of the interna-

'Paradise Lost' campaign image, 1992

tional trade in primates from the wild to the laboratory. The story gained national television coverage when it was broadcast by ITV's *World in Action* and a documentary video was produced, narrated by Joanna Lumley.

One success resulting from the campaign was the announcement in 1995 by the Home Office of a ban on the use of wild caught primates unless 'exceptional and specific justification' could be provided. It had been estimated that approximately 80 per cent of those primates captured in the wild died before they reached the laboratory. This not only reflected the extent of the trauma for a monkey trapped in the wild and shipped half way across the world to a research laboratory, but also indicated the enormous pressure being placed on the wild primate populations. As Britain was the world's second largest user of primates in research after the United States, it was hoped that this ban would have a significant impact on the future of the trade.

The response from the scientific community was

Genetic-engineering campaign image, 1995

the establishment of captive-bred breeding programmes to ensure its continued needs were met.
BUAV however had reservations about the validity of
some of the programmes established in source countries such as Indonesia where evidence suggested that
wild-caught primates were being exported as captive-
bred.

Another angle of the campaign was to put pressure
on those airlines which transported primates from the
wild to European and American research laboratories.
BUAV achieved enormous success in getting airlines to
withdraw from this trade. Many airlines pledged to end
their involvement in the primate trade in direct
response to the campaign including United Airlines,
one of the world's largest airlines.

In 1997 the Home Secretary also announced that
great apes (chimpanzees, orang-utans and gorillas)
would be excluded from research. This announcement
was highly significant. It was the first time that a category of animals had been excluded from research as 'a
matter of morality'. The Home Office stated that

*the cognitive and behavioural characteristics and quali-
ties of these animals mean it is unethical to treat them
as expendable for research.*[57]

Rapid growth in use of genetically-engineered animals

A new and increasing area of concern for BUAV in the
1990s was the rapid growth in the use of genetically-
engineered animals (animals which have had their
genetic make-up altered in some way). Genetic engineering carries with it a unique capacity to cause suffering as the results are often so unpredictable.
Genetically-manipulated animals are used for a number
of purposes; some are bred with specific genetic
defects to act as disease models for medical research,
others are used commercially as 'bio-reactors' to produce pharmaceuticals in their milk or blood, some are
used in the controversial area of xenotransplant
research (animal to human transplants). Cloning of animals has been the most recent revelation.

BUAV focused on the issue of patenting genetically-
engineered animals and its opposition to the 'onco-
mouse' patent became a test case at the European
Patent Office. Scientists at Harvard University who
developed a mouse designed to develop cancer had
been awarded the world's first animal patent in the
United States and in 1992 were also granted a patent
by the European Patent Office. BUAV, in conjunction
with Compassion in World Farming (CIWF), submitted
a legal opposition to the European Patent Office about
its decision to grant the patent. They argued firstly that
the production of these animals was 'contrary to morality' and therefore should be excluded from patentabili-
ty, and secondly that granting animal patents simply
provided a huge financial incentive to the practice.

BUAV also submitted reports to advisory bodies
which were considering the issue of xenotransplanta-
tion - the transplanting of organs from one species to
another. The most common example of this was the
development of genetically-engineered pigs, with
human DNA incorporated into their make-up, to act as
organ donors for human heart transplant patients.
Claims from scientists of a new and sustainable supply

Chimera, BUAV's genetic-engineering campaign mascot, protesting against the patenting of genetically-engineered animals at the Patent Office, Newport

Logo of the European Coalition to End Animal Experiments

of organs failed to address the ethical concerns surrounding this type of research.

Biotechnology generates unease, not only among those concerned with animal rights but also within the environmental movement which has huge concerns over the use of genetically-modified crops and the release of genetically-modified organisms into the environment. BUAV called for a moratorium on the genetic engineering and patenting of animals to allow for a period of genuine public education and debate.

Following on from the success of Vanity in publicising the issue of cosmetic testing, a new campaign mascot was designed for the campaign against genetic engineering. Chimera, a visual representation of the horrors of genetic engineering, was unveiled in 1995 at a protest outside the Patent Office in Newport, Gwent.

International campaigns - international exposés

The campaign to end cosmetic testing on animals was taken to a wider audience in the 1990s by the establishment of the European Coalition to End Cosmetic Tests On Animals. This was set up initially as a temporary coalition to lobby the European Parliament about cosmetic testing. However, the Coalition proved such a success that a decision was taken to continue the campaigning alliance. The European Coalition to End Animal Experiments (as it was renamed) is currently made up of 15 animal protection societies throughout Europe and, although an independent body, it continues to be led by BUAV.

As legislation is increasingly drafted and implemented at a European level it has been essential for BUAV to take its concerns to the European Union. The Intergroup on Animal Welfare was established in the 1980s to enable MEPs of all parties with a concern for animal issues to meet and discuss matters in the European Parliament and, in 1986, European Directive 86/609/EEC on animal experimentation was adopted. The terms of the Directive require the use of alternatives wherever 'reasonably and practically available' and places an obligation on scientists to use 'the minimum number of animals' and to minimise 'pain, suffering, distress or lasting harm'. BUAV has been able to use this European legislation to put pressure on countries that have been in breach of the legislation.

Molly, as she was found by BUAV's undercover investigator in Portugal and, later, after settling into her new home

In 1994 Portuguese laboratories were exposed for using stray cats and dogs which is clearly forbidden under the terms of the 1986 Directive. Molly, a stray dog, became a symbol of this campaign when she was rescued by BUAV and flown to a new life in this country courtesy of Iberia Airlines. Under increasing pressure from both the European Parliament and the European Commission, the Portuguese authorities conducted their own investigation and suspended research where there were cases of stray dogs being used. Portugal was instructed by the European Commission to implement Directive 86/609/EEC following continued public and political pressure.

Two years after the revelation of breaches in European Union law in Portugal a 'disturbing' trade in the use of stray cats and dogs was uncovered at the heart of the European Union. Scores of non-purpose-bred cats and dogs were uncovered by BUAV investigators in Belgian laboratories; many were found in conditions below the legal acceptable standard. At the Erasme University Hospital a number of dogs were seized by the authorities and were rehomed.

BUAV was 'extremely disappointed' at the response from the Belgian authorities and their failure to address a serious breach of legislation. Following their failure to take any action BUAV submitted a formal legal com-plaint to the European Commission in the hope of ensuring that the Directive would be enforced. During 1997, a record number of MEPs wrote to the European Commission in support of BUAV's complaint. In its response the Commission stated that it was checking the information supplied and 'will initiate infringement proceedings against Belgium if appropriate'.

In 1994 BUAV exposed disturbing scenes of animal experimentation in Poland and the Polish authorities were flooded with postcards of protest from BUAV members. In February 1995 Sarah Kite (by now Assistant Campaigns Director at BUAV) attended a press conference in Warsaw organised by the League for Nature Protection and also visited the offices of Lech Walesa to hand in a letter of protest from BUAV. A few weeks later a historic first-ever anti-vivisection march took place in Poland.

'Have a Heart' was the Valentine's Day message from BUAV to the Japanese authorities in February 1996. This followed an undercover investigation which exposed shocking evidence of cruel experiments. The animals were kept in appalling conditions and were in a state of total neglect. With legal protection in Japan almost non-existent BUAV called on the Japanese government to carry out its own investigation into laboratory conditions.

Undercover investigations

In 1992, undercover investigator Neil Fry worked as an animal technician at Wickham Laboratories in Hampshire for three months. Here he uncovered evidence of breaches of Home Office licence conditions and the falsification of test data. BUAV submitted a full report to the Home Office outlining all the areas of concern.

The Home Office followed up the report with its own inquiry which revealed 'a number of weaknesses in the company's procedures and practices'.[58] Wickham Laboratories was asked to replace the member of staff who had day-to-day responsibility for running the animal house, one personal licence was revoked and a number of other staff were warned about their future conduct. The Home Office enquiry found evidence of

poor local management, resulting in lax attitudes and practices among certain staff. These included a readiness to falsify test and environmental data on occasions.[59]

The success of the 'Paradise Lost' campaign was largely due to extensive evidence obtained by undercover investigators. Investigators worked in the countries of origin of the primates, including Indonesia, Mauritius and the Philippines. Another investigator, Terry Hill, worked at Britain's largest primate dealer, Shamrock Farm in Brighton. He then added the final link in the chain of supply of primates from the wild to the laboratory when he worked in the primate unit at Hazleton Research Laboratory in Harrogate.

Footage obtained undercover also helped to bring media attention to other campaigns such as 'Cosmetic Testing: It's In Your Hands'.

Huntingdon Life Sciences: it's a dog's life

In 1997 Huntingdon Life Sciences (HLS), formerly known as Huntingdon Research Centre, was penetrated once again, this time by independent undercover investigator Zoë Broughton. The evidence obtained by a hidden video camera caused an enormous public outcry when the shocking evidence of dogs being punched, slapped and abused was shown on Channel 4. This led to severe repercussions to HLS commercially (as pharmaceutical companies stopped giving the laboratory work) and financially (as its share value on the stock market plummeted). It also sent shock waves through the entire animal research industry.

The Home Office launched its own investigation and also referred the matter to the police to investigate possible criminal offences. HLS's licence was temporarily suspended and three members of staff dismissed. Two individuals were found guilty under the Protection of Animals Act 1911 of 'cruelly terrifying dogs'. However, their punishment of 60 hours' community service was condemned by BUAV as too 'soft' and for failing to set a deterrent against cruelty to laboratory animals.

Backed by MPs and celebrities BUAV was at the forefront of the campaign against HLS calling for its licence granted under the 1986 Act to be revoked and helping to maintain the issue in both the local and national media. A delegation of representatives from animal protection societies handed in a letter to the Home Office calling for a full and independent public inquiry. BUAV also submitted its own report to the Home Office and to the Animal Procedures Committee (advisers to the government on the 1986 Act) which detailed breaches of the Act and its related codes of practice.

HLS, in an apparent effort to curb the campaign against it, obtained an injunction against BUAV using the Protection from Harassment Act 1997. As its campaign against the laboratory had been entirely peaceful and legitimate, BUAV decided to challenge the injunction in the High Court and, in doing so, challenge the inappropriate way in which HLS had used the Act against it. BUAV not only had the injunction lifted but also welcomed the judge's important comments about use of the Act to curb the legitimate right to protest. BUAV was supported in this action by the human rights group Liberty.

The 1986 Act: 10 years on

Promoted as the 'toughest' legislation on animal experimentation in the world, 20 May 1996 saw the 10th anniversary of the introduction of the Animals (Scientific Procedures) Act 1986. The Animal Procedures Committee decided to review key aspects of the Act and BUAV was invited to submit evidence. BUAV criticised the current implementation and interpretation of the Act. In particular, it emphasised that trivial experiments such as cosmetic testing still continued despite a clause which requires that the 'likely adverse effects on the animal' should be weighed against the likely benefit of the experiment. In addition, legislative breaches based on evidence obtained by undercover investigations were highlighted as serious issues which the Home Office should address.

The Animal Procedures Committee published its interim review of the Act in August 1997. BUAV's response was one of disappointment. Although it welcomed measures such as those to increase the animal welfare interests on the Committee and to strengthen the Home Office inspectorate, it hopes that the completed review will be much more far-reaching.

BUAV: a century of campaigning against cruelty

On the eve of its 100th birthday in 1998, BUAV remembers with pride the words of its founder, Frances Power Cobbe, who

resolved never to go to bed at night leaving a stone unturned which might help to stop vivisection.

With Home Office statistics showing that in Great Britain 2,635,969 experimental procedures were carried out in 1997 on living animals, BUAV resolves that its work will continue until all animal experimentation has been abolished once and for all.

The British Union for the Abolition of Vivisection - a century of campaigning against cruelty.

Epilogue

In 1997 the British Union for the Abolition of Vivisection adopted, for the first time, a mission statement setting out the organisation's key aims and objectives.

- BUAV opposes animal experiments. We believe animals are entitled to respect and compassion which animal experiments deny them.

- BUAV campaigns peacefully for effective, lasting change by challenging attitudes and actions towards animals worldwide.

These statements provide BUAV with a progressive framework for all our campaigning activity into the next millennium and beyond.

Like many voluntary sector organisations, the raison d'être of BUAV is ultimately to help create a society where the organisation no longer needs to exist. Emma Hopley's book describes in fascinating detail the progress the organisation has made in combating animal experimentation.

We know it will be a long struggle to rid ourselves of this unethical and scientifically flawed practice. However, we have witnessed over the past 100 years a number of initiatives that have changed society's view about animal experimentation and brought about many practical and political changes to improve the lives of laboratory animals.

In 1997 a number of developments represented further significant and substantial steps. In particular, for the first time in the UK, it has been accepted that some tests are simply too trivial to justify animal suffering (cosmetic, alcohol and tobacco products). It is also the first time anywhere in the world that some 'non-human' animals have been excluded altogether from research - the great apes.

As we approach the new millennium we will build on these achievements and I am sure anyone reading this book will feel both informed and inspired.

BUAV
June 1998

References

CHAPTER 1
1   *The Abolitionist*. 16 September 1901; p 66.
2   *The Abolitionist*. 20 April 1904; p 2.
3   Westacott, E. *A Century of Vivisection and Anti-vivisection: A Study of Their Effect upon Science, Medicine and Human Life During the Past Hundred Years*. Ashingdon: The CW Daniel Company Ltd 1949: p 120.
4   *The Abolitionist*. 20 April 1904; p 4.
5   Westacott; p 65.
6   *Ibid* p 123.
7   *Ibid* p 204.

CHAPTER 2
8   BUAV half-yearly report for the six months ending 31 October 1898; p 1.
9   *The Abolitionist*. 15 May 1903; p 17.
10 *The Abolitionist*. 15 August 1903; p 56.
11 *The Abolitionist*. 20 April 1904; p 1.
12 *Ibid*; p 8.

CHAPTER 3
13 Vyvyan, John. *The Dark Face of Science*. London: Michael Joseph Ltd 1971: p 25.
14 BUAV annual report year ending May 1910; p 10.
15 *The Abolitionist*. 15 April 1907; p 3.
16 BUAV annual report year ending May 1909; p 9.
17 *The Abolitionist*. 14 August 1909; p 79.
18 Vyvyan; p 89.
19 *Ibid* p 89.
20 *Ibid* p 98.

CHAPTER 4
21 Vyvyan; p 60-61.
22 *Ibid* p 75.
23 *Ibid* p 75.
24 *The Abolitionist*. 15 May 1904; p 16-17.
25 Westacott; p 196.
26 *The Abolitionist*. 15 January 1907; p 90.
27 *The Abolitionist*. 15 April 1907; p 5.
28 *The Abolitionist*. 1 March 1913; p 51.

CHAPTER 5
29 Kidd, Beatrice E and Richards, M Edith. *Hadwen of Gloucester: Man, Medico, Martyr*. London: John Murray 1933: p 83.
30 *The Abolitionist*. 1 July 1922; p 90.
31 Westacott; p 444.
32 *The Abolitionist*. 2 July 1917; p 192.

CHAPTER 6
33 Ryder, Richard D. *Animal Revolution: Changing Attitudes Towards Speciesism*. Oxford: Basil Blackwell Ltd 1989: p 146.
34 *The Abolitionist*. 1 February 1923; p 17.
35 *The Abolitionist*. 1 August 1917; p 214.
36 *Ibid* p 212-213.
37 *The Abolitionist*. 1 July 1922; p 81.
38 *The Abolitionist*. 1 April 1927; p 47.
39 Lawrence, Christopher. 'Cinema Verité?: The Image of William Harvey's Experiments in 1928' in Rupke, Nicholaas, A [ed] *Vivisection in Historical Perspective*. London: Croom Helm Ltd 1987: p 301.
40 *Ibid* p 300.
41 Vyvyan; p 127.
42 *Ibid* p 127.

CHAPTER 7
43 *The Liberator*. Winter 1991; p 30.
44 *The Abolitionist*. 1 December 1924; p 151.
45 *The Liberator*. Winter 1991; p 30.

CHAPTER 8
46 Letter from BBC Assistant Director of Talks dated 22 April 1932. Reprinted in *The Abolitionist*. 1 June 1932; p 79.
47 *The Abolitionist*. 1 January 1935; p 2.

CHAPTER 9
48 *The Abolitionist*. July/August 1948; p 28.

CHAPTER 10
49 *The Abolitionist*. January/February 1943; p 7.
50 BUAV annual report year ending 30 April 1947; p 12.

CHAPTER 11
51 Quoted in BUAV's annual report year ending 30 April 1956; p 14.

CHAPTER 13
52 Vyvyan; p 177.
53 Ryder; p 243.
54 *The Anti-Vivisectionist*. July/August 1965; p 44.

CHAPTER 14
55 *AV Times*. May 1975; p 2.
56 BUAV annual report 1980; p 3.

CHAPTER 16
57 Lord Williams. Home Office Minister News Release; 6 November 1997.
58 Charles Wardle. Home Office News Release; 22 June 1993.
59 *Ibid*.